Family-Based Treatment for Young Ch

Family-Based Treatment for Young Children With OCD

Therapist Guide

Jennifer B. Freeman • Abbe Marrs Garcia

UNIVERSITY PRESS

2009

OXFORD
UNIVERSITY PRESS

Oxford University Press, Inc., publishes works that further
Oxford University's objective of excellence
in research, scholarship, and education.

Oxford   New York
Auckland   Cape Town   Dar es Salaam   Hong Kong   Karachi
Kuala Lumpur   Madrid   Melbourne   Mexico City   Nairobi
New Delhi   Shanghai   Taipei   Toronto

With offices in
Argentina   Austria   Brazil   Chile   Czech Republic   France   Greece
Guatemala   Hungary   Italy   Japan   Poland   Portugal   Singapore
South Korea   Switzerland   Thailand   Turkey   Ukraine   Vietnam

Published by Oxford University Press, Inc.
198 Madison Avenue, New York, New York 10016

www.oup.com

Oxford is a registered trademark of Oxford University Press

Freeman, Jennifer B.
Family-based treatment for young children with OCD :
therapist guide / Jennifer B. Freeman, Abbe Marrs Garcia.
    p.   ;   cm. — (Programs That Work)
Includes bibliographical references.
ISBN 978-0-19-537363-9
1. Obsessive-compulsive disorder in children—Treatment.   2. Cognitive therapy for children.
3. Parent and child.   4. Family psychotherapy.   I. Garcia, Abbe Marrs.   II. Title.
III. Series: Programs that work.
[DNLM: 1. Obsessive-Compulsive Disorder—therapy.   2. Child.   3. Family
Therapy—methods. WM 176 F869f 2008]
RJ506.O25F74 2008
618.92′891425—dc22
                                                            2008017743

About Programs*ThatWork*™

Stunning developments in health care have taken place over the last several years, but many of our widely accepted interventions and strategies in mental health and behavioral medicine have been brought into question by research evidence as not only lacking benefit but perhaps inducing harm. Other strategies have been proven effective using the best current standards of evidence, resulting in broad-based recommendations to make these practices more available to the public. Several recent developments are behind this revolution. First, we have arrived at a much deeper understanding of pathology, both psychological and physical, which has led to the development of new, more precisely targeted interventions. Second, our increased understanding of developmental issues allows a finer matching of interventions to developmental levels. Third, our research methodologies have improved substantially, such that we have reduced threats to internal and external validity, making the outcomes more directly applicable to clinical situations. Fourth, governments around the world and healthcare systems and policymakers have decided that the quality of care should improve, that it should be evidence-based, and that it is in the public's interest to ensure that this happens (Barlow, 2004; Institute of Medicine, 2001).

Of course, the major stumbling block for clinicians everywhere is the accessibility of newly developed evidence-based psychological interventions. Workshops and books can go only so far in acquainting responsible and conscientious practitioners with the latest behavioral healthcare practices and their applicability to individual patients. This new series, Programs*ThatWork*™, is devoted to communicating these exciting new interventions for children and their parents to clinicians on the frontlines of practice.

The manuals and workbooks in this series contain step-by-step detailed procedures for assessing and treating specific problems and diagnoses. But this series also goes beyond the books and manuals by providing ancillary materials that will approximate the supervisory process in assisting practitioners in the implementation of these procedures in their practice.

In our emerging healthcare system, the growing consensus is that evidence-based practice offers the most responsible course of action for the mental health professional. All behavioral healthcare clinicians deeply desire to provide the best possible care for their patients. In this series, our aim is to close the dissemination and information gap and make that possible.

This therapist guide describes a cognitive-behavioral family intervention for obsessive-compulsive disorder (OCD) in young children (ages 5–8). Successful treatment for early childhood–onset OCD must take into account the child's developmental stage and dependence on the family system. This guide gives instructions for incorporating parent involvement and tailoring sessions to the young child's cognitive and socioemotional levels. Exposure with response prevention (E/RP) is the main component of treatment, wherein the child is exposed to the feared situation, and the usual response (i.e., the ritual or avoidance behavior) is prevented until anxiety decreases. Every session works toward progressing up the hierarchy of E/RP tasks. A reward plan facilitates practicing E/RP at home. In addition, "parent tools" and "child tools" help families reduce and manage OCD symptoms. Parents learn how to use differential attention, modeling, and scaffolding to support their child. Children learn how to externalize ("boss back") OCD and use a feelings thermometer to rate anxiety. The corresponding workbook for families includes psychoeducation, reviews skills learned in therapy, and provides forms for homework. Clinicians will find this an invaluable guide for better serving the needs of young children with OCD and their families.

Anne Marie Albano, Editor-in-Chief
David H. Barlow, Editor-in-Chief
Programs *ThatWork* ™

References

Barlow, D. H. (2004). Psychological treatments. *American Psychologist, 59,* 869–878.

Institute of Medicine (2001). *Crossing the quality chasm: A new health system for the 21st century.* Washington, DC: National Academy Press.

In memory of Henreitta Leonard, our mentor.

Acknowledgments

We would like to thank Lisa Opipari, PhD, Gahan Fallone, PhD, John Piacentini, PhD, and John March, MD, for their thoughtful comments on the early drafts of this manual and for their involvement in the development of this project. We thank Lisa Coyne, PhD, for being a superb therapist, for showing us what a CBT program can really look like, and for pushing us to publish our manual. This work could not have happened without the help and perseverance of a talented staff of research assistants, including Chelsea Ale, Alexa Ogata, Janet Ng, Noah Berman, Mai Karitani Manchanda, Christina Fucci, and Lauren Miller. Finally, we gratefully thank the many children, families, and therapists with whom we have worked throughout the years for their contributions to the development and testing of this treatment program.

Contents

Chapter 1   *Introductory Information for Therapists*

Background Information and Purpose of This Program

This therapist manual describes a standardized cognitive-behavioral family intervention for young children (ages 5–8) with obsessive-compulsive disorder (OCD) and their parents. The overall focus of treatment is to provide parents and children with a set of "tools" to help them understand, manage, and reduce OCD symptoms. The family-based program consists of psychoeducation about OCD in young children, parent training, and exposure with response prevention (E/RP) for young children and their parents. This guide is intended for use by therapists (both psychologists and social workers) with experience in cognitive-behavioral therapy (CBT) with children. Specific previous experience with behavioral parent training techniques is not necessary, but often proves helpful in the implementation of the parent tools portion of this treatment program.

The corresponding workbook is designed to help families learn skills taught within therapy sessions and to assist with practice at home. It is recommended that the parent(s) be given a copy of the workbook to use with their child in and out of session.

Childhood-Onset Obsessive-Compulsive Disorder

Prevalence

Childhood-onset OCD is a chronic disturbance that affects as many as 2–3% of children (e.g., Valleni-Basile et al., 1994); point prevalence estimates indicate that between 0.5 and 1% of the pediatric population suffers from OCD (Flament et al., 1988). These figures may be underestimates of the true magnitude of the problem in children under the age of 9 years (herein referred to as "early childhood–onset OCD") because, in this age range, children's tendency to be secretive about OCD symptoms (Rapoport et al., 2000) may be coupled with developmentally based difficulty in articulating their concerns to others. Even when detected, OCD in young children appears to be undertreated.

Although OCD itself causes significant morbidity, the vast majority of children with OCD also develop additional psychiatric disorders (75–84% comorbidity) (Geller, Biederman, Griffin, Jones, & Lefkowitz, 1996). Common comorbid diagnoses include other anxiety disorders, tic disorders, disruptive behavior disorders (particularly attention deficit/hyperactivity disorder [ADHD] and oppositional defiant disorder [ODD]), and mood disorders. See Chapter 2 for more information on assessing comorbid diagnoses and differential diagnosis.

Symptoms

Symptoms of OCD in childhood are similar to those in older children, adolescents, and adults, and include recurrent and distressing thoughts, images, ideas, or impulses (obsessions) and mental acts or repetitive behaviors (compulsions) which are often performed to neutralize anxiety associated with obsessions (see Figure 1.1). In our work with early childhood–onset OCD, we found that checking and washing were the most common compulsions, and contamination fears and aggression were the most common obsessions (Garcia et al., in press).

Impairment

Childhood-onset OCD is associated with significant functional impairment in a number of critical domains. Furthermore, this impairment may compound over time to derail the acquisition and mastery of other important developmental milestones (Flament et al., 1990; Leonard,

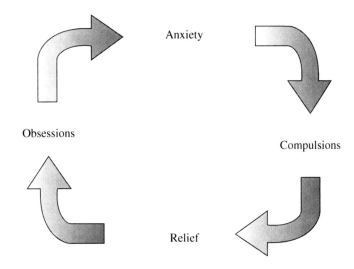

Figure 1.1
The OCD Cycle

Lenane, & Swedo, 1993; Piacentini, Bergman, Keller, & McCracken, 2003; Swedo, Rapoport, Leonard, Lenane, & Cheslow, 1989; Valderhaug & Ivarsson, 2005). If left untreated or if inadequately treated, young children have an increased likelihood that OCD will severely disrupt normative development, impair functioning, and extend into adulthood.

Diagnostic Criteria for Obsessive-Compulsive Disorder

The *Diagnostic and Statistical Manual of Mental Disorders, fourth edition, text revision* (*DSM-IV-TR*) (American Psychological Association, 2000) criteria for OCD are provided here. These criteria, which are the same for children and adults, must be met to qualify for a diagnosis of OCD. Although the criteria are the same, assessment of these symptoms in young children requires a developmentally sensitive approach and will be addressed further in Chapter 2.

A. Either obsessions or compulsions:
    Obsessions as defined by 1, 2, 3, and 4:

    1. recurrent and persistent thoughts, impulses or images that are experienced, at some time during the disturbance, as intrusive

and inappropriate and that cause marked anxiety or distress

2. the thoughts, impulses, or images are not simply excessive worries about real-life problems

3. the person attempts to ignore or suppress such thoughts, impulses, or images, or to neutralize them with some other thought or action

4. the person recognizes that the obsessional thoughts, impulses, or images are a product of his or her mind

Compulsions as defined by 1 and 2:

1. repetitive behaviors (e.g., hand washing, ordering, checking) or mental acts (e.g., praying, counting, repeating words silently) that the person feels driven to perform in response to an obsession, or according to rules that must be applied rigidly

2. the behaviors or mental acts are aimed at preventing or reducing distress or preventing some dreaded event or situation; however, these behaviors or mental acts either are not connected in a realistic way with what they are designed to neutralize or prevent or are clearly excessive.

B.   At some point during the course of the disorder, the person has recognized that the obsessions or compulsions are excessive or unreasonable. Note: *This does not apply to children.*

C.   The obsessions or compulsions cause marked distress, are time-consuming (take more than one hour a day), or significantly interfere with the person's normal routine, occupations (or academic functioning), or usual social activities or relationships.

D.   If another Axis I disorder is present, the content of the obsessions or compulsions is not restricted to it (e.g., preoccupation with food in the presence of an eating disorder, hair pulling in the presence of trichotillomania, concern with appearance in the presence of body dysmorphic disorder).

E.   The disturbance is not the result of the direct physiological effects of a substance (e.g., a drug of abuse, a medication) or a general medical condition.

This manual was developed for use in a federally funded treatment development study to examine the efficacy of a family-based intervention for early childhood–onset OCD. The use of a cognitive-behavioral family intervention is the result of our observations that young children with OCD need significant family support in order to address their OCD symptoms and that interventions need to be very sensitive to the developmental capacity of the patient. Additionally, we have found that parents need specific tools (e.g., behavior modification strategies and increased awareness of their own anxiety) to help their children effectively implement the E/RP component of the treatment program at home. For example, very young children with OCD often have less intrinsic motivation to change patterns of behavior and need more help to understand the benefits of changes that they have made. Therefore, parents must practice communicating with their child about thoughts and emotions and must actively implement behavioral strategies to increase the child's motivation for change.

Portions of this manual have been adapted from existing treatment programs with the permission of the authors. The following manuals and authors have helped immensely in the development of this treatment program: *OCD in Children and Adolescents: A Cognitive Behavioral Treatment Manual* (March & Mulle, 1998) and *Individual CBT and Family (ERP/Family) Treatment: A Multicomponent Treatment Program for Children and Adolescents with Obsessive-Compulsive Disorder* (Piacentini, Jacobs, & Maidment, 1998).

Tailoring to Young Children

Our family-based CBT for young children with OCD draws on extant approaches used with older children, but this treatment program contains novel elements that have been specifically tailored to young children aged 5–8 with OCD. These elements include (1) attention to developmental stage and concomitant levels of cognitive and socioemotional skills, and (2) awareness of a child's involvement in and dependence on a family system. First, this program addresses the cognitive and socioemotional levels of younger children through the use of very specific, concrete, and child-friendly examples. These examples are used to

1. provide the rationale for E/RP (e.g., by making connections to other fears the child has conquered or explaining that it is like taking a medicine that tastes "yucky" but makes you better),

2. distinguish obsessional thoughts from other, non-intrusive recurring cognitions or images (e.g., by explaining that these thoughts are different than having a song stuck in your head or thinking about a scary movie you have seen), and

3. identify the connection between obsessional thoughts and subsequent compulsions (e.g., by explaining that obsession is like a "worry monster" that tells you things it wants you to do).

Parent Involvement

Throughout treatment, parents are included in structured, specific ways to address issues of family functioning and parenting. The inclusion of parents serves a threefold purpose. First, parents are trained as coaches for their children, and play a key role in shaping treatment and ensuring adherence and motivation outside of session. Second, including parents directly addresses parents' tendency to accommodate their child's OCD behavior. Third, treatment has an "exposure" function for parents as well, as they are asked to tolerate their own distress in the face of assisting their children with often upsetting exposure exercises and homework tasks (Pollack & Carter, 1999).

We also addressed the issue that this may be a family's first contact with the mental health system. Families are often unsure whether their children's symptoms are reflective of normative, if disturbing, developmental phases that they will "outgrow," or whether these symptoms herald clinically serious issues. Moreover, entry into treatment is daunting for parents, who may be concerned that OCD symptoms at such a young age are perhaps insurmountable. Finally, given their child's developmental stage and the relatively greater demands that young children place on families, parents may have difficulty attending sessions, managing child oppositionality and treatment resistance, and consistently completing homework tasks.

Evidence Base for This Treatment Program

Preliminary randomized controlled treatment data from a NIMH-funded treatment development study using the treatment program described in this manual (NIH R21 MH60669) are reviewed below. Results indicate that children with early childhood–onset OCD benefit from a treatment approach tailored to their developmental needs and family context and that family-based CBT was effective in reducing OCD symptoms and in helping a large number of children achieve a clinical remission. In this study, the intent-to-treat (ITT) sample included 42 children ranging in age from 4 to 8 years (mean, 7.11; SD 1.26) and their parents. Although the treatment and study were designed for children ages 5–8, we did enroll two children who were consented at age 4 but turned 5 during the course of treatment.

In order to participate in the study, children met the following inclusion criteria at the time of evaluation:

(1) a primary *DSM-IV* diagnosis of OCD;

(2) symptom duration of at least 3 months;

(3) ages 5–8; and (4) at least one parent who was able to consistently attend treatment sessions.

The exclusion criteria were the following:

(1) other primary psychiatric disorder or co-primary/secondary diagnosis that required initiation of other active treatment;

(2) pervasive developmental disorder(s), including Asperger's syndrome; documented mental retardation; thought disorder or psychotic symptoms; and conduct disorder;

(3) acute suicidality;

(4)   concurrent psychotherapy for OCD or behavioral parent training;

(5)   treatment with psychiatric medication for depression or mood stabilization;

(6)   treatment with psychiatric medication for OCD, ADHD, and/or tic disorders that was not stable (6 weeks at a stable dose prior to evaluation);

(7)   previous failed trial of CBT for OCD (defined as 10 sessions of formalized E/RP); and

(8)   met research criteria for the Pediatric Autoimmune Neuropsychiatric Disorders Associated with Streptococcal Infection (PANDAS) subtype of OCD/tics or on antibiotic prophylaxis for PANDAS (owing to concerns that apparent treatment gains could be a result of an episodic symptom course).

The sample was primarily Caucasian (80% Caucasian, 2% Hispanic, 2% Asian or Pacific Islander, 2% Native American, 2% multiracial, and 12% no response/unknown) and middle class (although 8% of the sample was below the poverty level), with roughly equal gender distribution (57% female).

With regard to comorbid diagnoses (as measured by the K-SADS), 54.8% had comorbid internalizing diagnoses and 35.7% had comorbid externalizing diagnoses, 9.5% had a tic disorder, and 19% had ADHD. Also, 14.3% were taking a selective serotonin reuptake inhibitor (SSRI) for OCD and 4.8% were taking a psychostimulant for ADHD. As indexed by the baseline Children's Yale-Brown Obsessive-Compulsive Scale (CY-BOCS) ($M = 22.36$; $SD = 4.17$; range $= 11 - 32$) scores, the sample had moderately severe OCD symptoms. The mean age of onset of the sample was 4.99 ($SD = 1.27$) and 16% ($n = 7$) of the children had previous treatment (either medication and/or psychotherapy).

The CBT treatment was compared to a relaxation treatment (RT) program. Both treatment protocols (CBT and RT) consisted of 12 sessions delivered over the course of 14 weeks. All study therapists were clinical psychology interns, postdoctoral fellows, or clinical psychologists with expertise in the application of behavioral therapy with anxiety disorders, parent behavior management training, and relaxation and family-based treatment. Doctoral-level clinical psychologists (J.B.F and A.M.G.) provided all training and supervision. Training included didactic instruction, familiarization with the treatment manuals, and role-playing of treatment procedures. All therapy sessions were videotaped and discussed in weekly group supervision.

Of the 42 randomized patients, 31 (74%) completed acute treatment (through week 14). Five patients (12%) were provided rescue treatments to address emergent clinical concerns that could not be managed within the treatment protocols. Of these, one patient (in the RT condition) had OCD symptoms worsen and required additional out-of-protocol treatment and the remaining four patients had another diagnosis become primary (eating, depressive, separation anxiety, or tic disorder). Six (14%) patients dropped out of the study. Of these, one moved to another city, one was unhappy with the outcome of randomization, two had family health problems (parent, grandparent) that interfered with ability to attend treatment, and two completed the treatment but not the last assessment. The attrition rate for this study ($n = 9$ or 26%) is consistent with that found in other pediatric anxiety treatment studies (22–27%; 13–38% CBT; 13–30% control)(Kendall et al., 1997; Last, Hansen, & Franco, 1998; Pina, Silverman, Weems, Kurtines, & Goldman, 2003; Silverman et al., 1999). The mean (median) numbers of completed CBT and RT sessions were 10.86 (12) for CBT and 11.1 (12) for RT.

There were no differences between completers ($n = 31$) and noncompleters ($n = 11$) on age, baseline CY-BOCS severity, race, gender, socioeconomic status, or comorbidity. There were also no differences between children randomized to CBT ($n = 22$) and those randomized to RT ($n = 20$) on these variables.

A series of independent sample t-tests show that the CBT and RT groups did not differ on any of the baseline child or parent psychopathology measures, including parent-rated measures of child OCD, anxiety, and externalizing symptoms; global measures of child OCD, impairment, depression, and anxiety; parent self-rated psychiatric symptoms, depression, and OCD; or general family functioning.

Using the ITT sample, 11 of 22 (50%) participants randomized to CBT were classified as achieving clinical remission on the CY-BOCS (defined as a post-treatment CY-BOCS score ≤ 12) after 12 weeks of treatment, as compared with only 4 of 20 (20%) participants in the RT group. This difference in response rates was statistically and clinically significant ($\chi^2(1) = 4.11$, $p < 0.05$; $OR = 4.00$, (95% CI, 1.00, 15.87), $NNT = 3$). Using the completer sample, 11 of 16 (69%) participants randomized to CBT were classified on the CY-BOCS as achieving clinical remission, compared with only 3 of 15 (20%) participants in the RT group. This difference (49%) was statistically and clinically significant ($\chi^2(1) = 7.43$, $p < .01$; $OR = 8.80$, (95% CI, 1.69, 45.76), $NNT = 2$).

The results of this preliminary work were very encouraging and indicated that children experiencing early childhood–onset OCD indeed benefit from a treatment approach that is uniquely tailored to their developmental needs and family context. The CBT program was effective both in reducing OCD symptoms and, more importantly, in helping a large number of children achieve clinical remission, as measured by the CY-BOCS. As part of this study, we were able to demonstrate feasibility of recruiting and treating, as well as collecting data about, young children with OCD. We were able to show the tolerability and acceptability of the program to children and families (Kraemer & Kupfer, 2006), as well as the feasibility of combining family work and parent training skills alongside E/RP for OCD.

Other Studies on CBT for OCD

The largest completed randomized controlled trial (RCT) to date of CBT for OCD in children evaluated the efficacy of CBT and sertraline (Zoloft®) in comparison with CBT alone, sertraline alone, and a pill placebo for a duration of 12 weeks. The CBT manual included both exposure and response prevention in addition to cognitive interventions such as psychoeducation about OCD. Results indicated that patients treated with CBT either alone or in combination with sertraline showed a substantial improvement in OCD symptoms (Pediatric OCD Treatment Study Team [POTS], 2004). These findings suggest that children and adolescents with OCD should begin treatment with CBT alone or CBT in combination with an SSRI, depending on severity and comorbidity. Although children as young as age seven have been included in prior RCTs of E/RP for OCD such as the POTS study, they have been underrepresented relative to older children and adolescents and the treatments have been primarily individual therapy models.

What is Exposure With Response Prevention?

E/RP is the behavioral treatment of choice for OCD in both adults and children (Abramowitz, Whiteside, & Deacon, 2005), but other than the results of our study presented earlier younger children have been underrepresented in those samples relative to older children and adolescents. In E/RP, the patient is exposed to the feared situation, and the response (i.e., the ritual or avoidance behavior) is prevented until anxiety decreases. For example, the child with contamination fears and washing rituals may be asked to touch items in the garbage and then not be allowed to wash his or her hands. Patients gradually learn that their anxious response decreases over time and that with prolonged exposure to the stimulus the anxiety can be reduced without performing compulsions (see Figure 1.2).

Exposure itself can be either imaginal or in vivo, and most commonly progresses in a graded manner according to a symptom hierarchy of increasingly anxiety-producing stimuli. The patient and therapist work together in early sessions to generate items for the hierarchy (e.g., by listing all symptoms) and rate the severity of anxiety on a scale. This collaboration serves to decrease the child's fear of the unknown and allows him or her to gain mastery. Although new items are frequently added to the hierarchy and anxiety ratings altered, the list ideally represents the total picture of the patient's OCD symptomatology and provides a model of how treatment will progress over time.

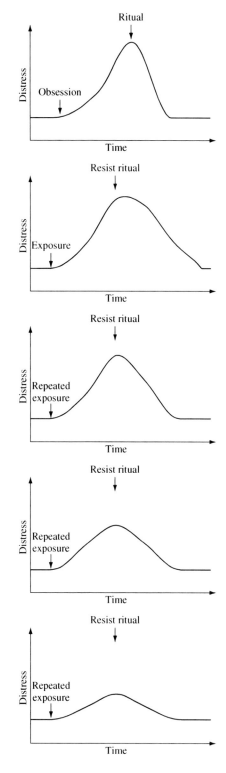

Figure 1.2

CBT Model of Exposure with Response Prevention for OCD

Risks and Benefits of This Treatment Program

The benefits of this treatment program have been outlined earlier, including attention to the developmental needs and family context of younger children with OCD, demonstrated remission rates above that of another active family-based treatment (RT), and tolerability and acceptability to children and families.

Although we do not think there are specific risks associated with this treatment program, it is important to acknowledge that CBT programs are not for everyone. Patient and family preference plays an important role in determining the appropriate treatment or the timing of treatment and this preference must not be underestimated. Cognitive-behavioral treatment is challenging for children and, in this particular program, for parents as well. The treatment requires that children talk about difficult topics (i.e., their OCD symptoms) and face difficult situations (i.e., exposure to anxiety-provoking stimuli). Parents too must learn to tolerate their own anxiety about watching their child become anxious. The treatment requires a considerable time commitment in terms of time spent in sessions and more importantly time spent at home on homework tasks. Additionally, this treatment is far more effective when families are engaged and motivated. We feel that it is not helpful for families to engage in this treatment program if they are not committed to making some changes. In situations where both children and parents are resistant to treatment on an ongoing basis, we often advise such families to take a break from treatment and try again in the future. This is important because we do not want children and families to decide that CBT "doesn't work," when it is other factors that are not allowing the child and/or family to fully benefit from the CBT program.

Alternative Treatments

There are no specific alternative treatments available for young children between the ages of 5 and 8 with OCD; however, treatments have been developed for older children with OCD (March & Mulle, 1998; Piacentini, Langley, & Roblek, 2007). There are often community providers with expertise in treating young children, but these treatments may or may not be cognitive-behavioral programs.

The Role of Medications

The Expert Consensus Guidelines, the AACAP Practice Parameters for OCD, and results from the POTS study (Pediatric OCD Treatment Study Team [POTS], 2004) recommend starting treatment in children with CBT, or CBT plus an SSRI, depending on severity and comorbidity. Given that this treatment is targeted toward younger children with OCD, many patients are new to any form of treatment and parents are less willing to try medication as a first-line treatment. However, many children on medication have participated in this treatment program and it is certainly recommended for children who are taking medication for their OCD (as well as for other disorders). There are no adaptations that are necessary to the program if a child is taking medication. To date, there has not been any investigation of this treatment program in comparison to a medication-only treatment condition.

Outline of This Treatment Program

The treatment protocol consists of 12 sessions delivered over the course of 14 weeks (see Table 1.1). The first 10 sessions are delivered weekly, with one-week intervals between the last three sessions. The first two sessions (90 min) are conducted with parents alone, with the remaining sessions (60 min) conducted jointly with both parents and children. The treatment consists of

1. psychoeducation,

2. parent education (parent tools), and

3. cognitive strategies and E/RP (child tools).

This manual outlines the sequence and required components of the treatment procedures and activities. Although the manual contains many sample dialogues, specific explanations, and methods for implementing treatment, components will necessarily depend on the age and

Table 1.1 Treatment Schedule

Session	Week	Participants	Treatment components*
1	1	Parents only	PE
2	2	Parents only	PE
3	3	Parents and child	PE; PT: Differential attention
4	4	Parents and child	CT: Bossing back; E/RP; PT: Ignoring
5	5	Parents and child	CT: Cognitive restructuring; E/RP; PT: Modeling
6	6	Parents and child	CT: Cognitive restructuring/hierarchy; E/RP; PT: Scaffolding
7	7	Parents and child	CT: E/RP; PT: Scaffolding
8	8	Parents and child	CT: E/RP; Portability
9	9	Parents and child	CT: E/RP; PT: Portability
10	10	Parents and child	CT: E/RP, Review; PT: Review
11	12	Parents and child	CT: E/RP; PT: Relapse prevention
12	14	Parents and child	Review and party

*PE = psychoeducation; CT = child tools; PT = parent tools

developmental resources of the child, the specific symptoms, and the nature of family functioning and support. This will remain a dynamic process throughout treatment. In our experience, 14 weeks of treatment is sufficient for most children in this program; however, the exact number of treatment sessions required is highly dependent on the overall clinical picture of the child and family, including the severity of the child's OCD, comorbid psychiatric diagnoses, concurrent family stressors, and family functioning.

Psychoeducation

The goals of the psychoeducation component are

1. to provide education about the neurobiology of OCD,

2. to correct misattributions about OCD,

3. to differentiate between OCD and non-OCD behaviors, and

4. to describe the treatment program in detail.

Parent Tools

The goal of this component is to provide parents with a set of "tools" that will be used throughout treatment to increase their child's motivation for change and to more effectively manage their child's OCD symptoms. These tools may indirectly help parents manage non-OCD problem behaviors as well. The central parent "tools" include

1. differential attention (behavior or response that is reinforced increases in frequency, while alternative response or behavior becomes less frequent),

2. modeling (parents behave in a certain way and child copies parental behavior), and

3. scaffolding (parent guides child's emotion regulation in response to an event or situation and child ultimately internalizes response as self-regulation, leading to independence).

We believe that when used together, these parent tools provide the foundation for successful implementation of OCD treatment in this age group. All parent tools will be discussed and rehearsed in session and then practiced at home as part of weekly homework assignments.

Cognitive Strategies and E/RP

The goal of the cognitive strategies component is to provide children and parents with some basic and developmentally appropriate "tools" to implement E/RP. These tools include

1. learning how to externalize ("boss back") OCD, and

2. using a feelings thermometer to rate anxiety.

The goal of the E/RP component is to have parents and children work together to develop a hierarchy and implement E/RP. The basic goal of E/RP is to gradually expose the child to the situations that are most uncomfortable until fear decreases on its own without the performance of rituals (the process of habituation). Home-based practice of E/RP will also be facilitated by the reward program.

Clinical Considerations and Adaptations

Flexibility With Younger Children

Therapist flexibility is expected in the utilization of the manual. For example, the order of presentation of topics within a given session may need to be altered to best meet the needs of a child or family. In the case of some children (particularly 5–6 year olds), it may be necessary to complete the portions of the session that require the child to be most active (e.g., "child tools") early in the hour. Alternatively, if parents come into the session with a particular family or parenting concern, then it may make sense to start with that section. Another example concerns the reward program. Behavioral reinforcement with sticker charts or other rewards is often very effective in increasing the child's motivation for change, but some anxious children can become so focused on the contingencies that it begins to interfere with their activities and family functioning. Overall, the goal is to complete all session elements in a manner that best matches the needs of the child and family.

Another way in which therapists need to be flexible in this treatment program is with regard to child resistance to engage in treatment, and more specifically resistance to engage in E/RP. Because younger children will likely have difficulty articulating specific reasons for resistance, it is important to use other information from parents, observational information from the child, and clues from past sessions to determine what might be causing problems with a given task. When therapists and parents have the sense that child resistance is related to an anxiety-based theme, it is often appropriate and helpful to decrease the level of difficulty of the E/RP task and review the child and parent tools that have been learned to date.

When therapists and parents feel that child resistance is more related to the child being oppositional, this is often complicated. There are some children who understand the treatment program and for a host of reasons do not want to participate or comply. In these cases, it is often possible to make alterations to the reward program (e.g., a tangible, immediate reward) and/or set up other contingencies to increase participation. It is very important, however, to look out for situations in which children seem to be oppositional because of a lack of understanding of the rationale for treatment. In these cases, it is very important to work to make sure that children understand at least something about why they are being asked to engage in E/RP.

A potential pitfall is a situation in which the therapist and parents do this treatment "to a child" rather than "with a child." In this age group of younger children, it is certainly the case that patients are rarely choosing to engage in treatment on their own accord. It is crucial that therapists be aware of the potential for coercion and make appropriate changes to the course of treatment if necessary. Although it is possible to keep pushing a child to do E/RP (particularly at the lower levels of the hierarchy), the value of this is questionable. If children are forced into doing this treatment against their will, it is likely to cause trouble later in this treatment program as well as in future attempts to do CBT (i.e., parents and family may have a false belief that CBT does not work). Our mission in the treatment program is to intervene early, but it is important that children are ready for treatment. There are indeed times when it is necessary to stop this program and try another treatment model or even stop treatment all together. This can be difficult for parents to understand, but it is an important component of treatment. The goal of this treatment is to create a team in which the child, parents, and therapist work together against OCD and not a situation in which parents and therapist are working against OCD and the child.

Specific Adaptations With Younger Children

Specific adaptations also may be required for younger children owing to the fact that they generally have less sophisticated emotion awareness and expression skills than older children. Such developmental differences are likely to affect the acquisition and application of skills that are integral to CBT, including the understanding of abstract concepts such as treatment rationale, the development of fear hierarchies, the use of rating systems and/or feeling thermometers, and understanding of reward systems.

For example, rating systems may need to be simplified (e.g., faces rather than numbers) or adapted (e.g., butterflies in the tummy, carrying heavy bricks) based on an individual child (see examples in Chapter 5). For some children, therapists and/or parents must use behavioral cues to estimate anxiety reactions rather than relying on the child's report from a rating scale. Part of the treatment involves training the parents to be able to identify more subtle cues and to break situations down for their child to help the child gradually learn to give more accurate ratings.

With regard to the reward program (which is discussed in detail in Session 2), it is important to adapt a reward system to the needs and abilities of both children and parents. Depending on the specific child and the situation, we may alter the frequency and type of reward. For example, for an older child, it is often possible to provide a reward for engaging or not engaging in a behavior for a larger amount of time (i.e., resisting hand-washing for an entire day), whereas for a younger child, it is important to break the day up into smaller time-periods (e.g., before lunch, after lunch, and after dinner). A related concept has to do with rewarding a group of behaviors (e.g., touching contaminant, resisting hand-washing, and not asking reassurance-seeking questions) which might be possible with an older child, but quite difficult with a younger child. With younger children, we would instead propose breaking up tasks into subsets of behavior and rewarding each component separately. The type of reward and the timing of the reinforcement are also important. Older children often do well with reward systems in which they earn stickers, chips, or other less immediately intrinsically reinforcing items that they can exchange for a tangible reinforcer at a later point in time (i.e., at the end of the day or the end of the week). Younger children may need an immediate tangible reinforcer (e.g., a tiny prize immediately following an exposure rather than a gold star). Finally, all of these changes to a reward system are dependent on parents being able to implement this more detailed system. We feel that it is imperative that a reward program be tied to a child's developmental level, but also that it is feasible for the family to execute. It is important for the therapist to talk with families about what a reward program will require and what the family feels able to accomplish on a daily basis.

Time Allotted

With the exception of Sessions 1 and 2 (which are designed for parents alone), both parents and children are expected to be present for all sessions. Keep in mind that the critical work of therapy will likely be done at home, outside of the sessions, and parents need to be prepared to coach their child in practicing skills. Therefore, parents must understand the skills that are introduced and why they are important to treatment. Therapists should act in a way that facilitates this understanding, which may require meeting with the parents without the child in the room. Nevertheless, anxious children may at times be more comfortable discussing their thoughts and feelings without their parents present, and therapists should remain sensitive to these needs and act accordingly, scheduling times for private interactions with a child if necessary. Certain components of therapy (e.g., parent tools) may require more or less time in each session depending on the needs of the family. Therapists will need to use their own clinical judgment to make these determinations.

Therapy Process Issues

Finally, "therapy process" issues will be identified in every session. These are themes for the therapist to consider and weave in throughout the session to enhance the focus on the specific issues being addressed. We distinguish these "process elements" from other session components because we have found that they are issues that cut across specific items on the agenda and they tend to be emotionally charged. For both of these reasons, we have found that it is preferable to work with them more organically—drawing them out as they arise naturally during the course of the session.

The accompanying workbook corresponds to this therapist guide and contains important information for families. Monitoring forms, exposure practice records, reward charts, and session homework sheets are also provided in the workbook. Optimally, the workbook will be brought to each session so that families can report on their work from the week, which may include symptom tracking, specific homework tasks, and monitoring of progress on a reward chart. Additionally, the workbook is meant to be used outside of sessions to reinforce skills and direct homework practice.

The workbook is addressed to parents, but includes material for children. Given the young age of the children targeted in this treatment program, parents will necessarily guide children through the content of the workbook. Rather than being structured session by session, the workbook is organized by theme: introduction to treatment, therapy process issues, parent tools, child tools, E/RP, and relapse prevention. Families should be encouraged to review the relevant sections of the workbook after each session.

Chapter 2 *Assessment*

Careful clinical assessment is an important step before beginning this treatment program for young children with obsessive-compulsive disorder (OCD). Prior to specific evaluation of a child's OCD symptoms, it is important to complete a thorough clinical assessment of the child's functioning across multiple domains. Clinical assessment is crucial in order to determine that OCD is in fact the child's primary disorder and to recognize comorbid diagnoses. As we discuss in this chapter, the types of instruments that are used or the kinds of evaluation conducted with a younger child are not completely distinct from what one would do with an older child. However, the ways in which questions are framed, the use of developmentally appropriate probes, and the format of the evaluation (i.e., with parents and child together) are different to a certain extent.

OCD Versus Developmentally Appropriate Behavior

Clinicians should first consider whether the child's recurrent thoughts or repetitive behaviors are developmentally appropriate. Developmental rituals of childhood are normal at certain ages, and they may be performed in a stereotypic or rule-bound fashion, which can make them difficult to differentiate from OCD rituals. Most children exhibit ritualistic or superstitious behaviors at some point during their development. These behaviors also tend to worsen during times of transition or stress (e.g., going to school or birth of a sibling). OCD rituals are usually more dramatic, persistent, and distressing than developmentally typical rituals (Evans et al., 1997; Leonard, Goldberger, Rapoport, Cheslow, & Swedo, 1990). For example, children who engage in developmentally typical rituals are much more likely to "give up" or "go along" with breaking a ritual when pressed, in contrast to a child with OCD who is much less likely to give up without protest and more significant distress. However, it is not always easy to differentiate the two kinds of rituals, and sometimes, normal ritualistic behavior can worsen over time and become more like OCD. Chapter 3 includes information on normal ritualistic behavior for different ages.

Differential and Comorbid Diagnoses

With regard to differential diagnosis, several other childhood disorders include obsessional features and compulsive behaviors. Stereotypies in autistic spectrum disorders may resemble OCD rituals in that the former are repetitive formalized behaviors. However, stereotypies are usually simple, do not appear to be preceded by an obsession, and are not ego-dystonic. The frequent association of OCD with tic disorders (Holzer et al., 1994; Leckman et al., 1994; Leonard et al., 1992; Pauls et al., 1986) requires that rituals and tics be distinguished because each requires different treatments. Treatment for tic disorders is addressed in a book in the TTW series, *Managing Tourette's Syndrome: A Behavioral Intervention for Children and Adults, Therapist Guide* (Woods et al., 2008).

Although motor tics can be preceded by a sensation or an "urge," they are typically not initiated by a thought or accompanied by anxiety (Leckman & Peterson, 1993). Obsessions and rituals can also be seen in depressive and other anxiety disorders, eating disorders, somatoform disorders, and impulse-control disorders. Finally, if the obsessions or compulsions are particularly bizarre, and seen by the patient as reasonable, a diagnosis of psychosis may be considered (although this is extremely rare in young children).

Once the diagnosis of OCD is suspected, it is not uncommon for there to be significant comorbidity, even in young children. Diagnoses that commonly occur with OCD include other anxiety disorders, tic disorders, disruptive behavior disorders (particularly attention deficit/hyperactivity disorder and oppositional defiant disorder), and mood disorders. In research studies, the task of differential diagnosis and establishing comorbid diagnoses is often accomplished through structured diagnostic interviews such as the Kiddie Schedule for Affective Disorders and Schizophrenia (KSADS; Kaufman et al., 1997) and the Anxiety Disorders Interview Schedule for Children (ADIS-C; Silverman & Albano, 1996). However, in clinical practice, this is often not feasible (or necessary) and a thorough clinical interview is appropriate.

Recommended Measures

With regard to the evaluation of young children with OCD for this treatment program, we do recommend two standardized measures: the Children's Yale-Brown Obsessive-Compulsive Scale (CY-BOCS) and the Family Accommodation and Impact Scale-Child (FAIS-C).

Children's Yale-Brown Obsessive-Compulsive Scale (CY-BOCS)

The CY-BOCS (Scahill et al., 1997) is a well-known 10-item semistructured clinician-rated interview that merges data from clinical observation and parent and child report. It is adapted from the adult Y-BOCS (Goodman, Price, Rasmussen, Mazure, Delgado et al., 1989; Goodman, Price, Rasmussen, Mazure, Fleischmann et al., 1989). It assesses OCD symptoms and severity. Obsessions and compulsions are rated on 0–4-point scales on five dimensions (time, interference, distress, resistance, and control). The CY-BOCS yields a total obsessions score (0–20), a total compulsion score (0–20), and a combined total score (0–40). Developmentally sensitive anchors and probes have been developed. Adequate reliability and validity, as well as sensitivity to change after treatment, have been demonstrated in pharmacological and behavioral therapy studies. The literature supports the use of the measure in children as young as 6 years (March & Leonard, 1998) and has been used successfully with 5-year-olds in our research program. The measure is appropriate for use with younger children, older children, and adolescents, but as we discuss later in the chapter, it is important to use it in a developmentally appropriate manner in this population. A CY-BOCS symptom checklist is included in an appendix.

Family Accommodation and Impact Scale-Child (FAIS-C)

The Family Accommodation and Impact Scale-Child (FAIS-C) is a clinician-rated interview designed to be administered to parents of children with OCD. The interview is designed to assess a range of accommodating behaviors and the impact of child symptoms on parents and family members of children with OCD. The FAIS-C is based on the original Family Accommodation Scale (FAS; Calvocoressi et al., 1999), which is a standardized clinician-rated interview used to assess accommodating behaviors in relatives of adult OCD patients. Questions from the FAS have been modified slightly for use with young children with the approval of the author, and additional items assessing the impact of the child's symptoms on family functioning have been added. The method of inquiring about impact was adapted from The Impact on Family Scale (Stein & Riessman, 1978). The FAS has adequate reliability and validity; however, the FAIS-C has not been validated to date. For the purposes of this treatment program, the goal of this measure is to help the therapist gain understanding before the start of treatment about the ways in which the family is affected by and plays a role in the child's OCD. A copy of the FAIS-C is included in an appendix of this guide.

Adaptations for Younger Children

In general, the younger the children are, the more difficulty they will have understanding questions that relate to their thoughts. They also will have more difficulty understanding concepts such as estimating, averaging, and time. In addition, using concrete examples will be necessary to obtain self-report information about their symptoms and behavior. Parents can be helpful in generating recent examples in which children may have demonstrated the symptom(s) in question. Parents also can often be helpful with rephrasing clinician's questions so that their child understands what is being asked. Some parents do this without prompting. Other parents are happy to help with translating the question if the clinician asks, for example, "Can you help me ask Mary this question in a way that she understands what I'm asking?"

The clinician should also be aware that time must be used wisely to balance inquiry with maintaining the child's attention. The clinician must be judicious in the management of inquiry into a particular topic, balancing the need to obtain better information from the child and parent with the need to complete the entire interview. For example, if too much time is spent evaluating obsessions, the child might be fatigued making it difficult to get much information to evaluate specific compulsions or to differentiate OCD-related compulsions from other repetitive behaviors such as tics.

Procedural Differences for Younger Children

While orienting the child and parent to the assessment process, it is very important to gauge their understanding of the terms "obsessions" and "compulsions" and to differentiate these symptoms from other symptoms that are similar or even dissimilar (i.e., parents commonly lump all symptoms together across OCD as well as other comorbid diagnoses). It is helpful to first have the parents and child report on the symptoms that have caused them to present for treatment and to listen for the particular language or words they use to describe the symptoms that the clinician understands to be obsessions and compulsions. Then, after identifying these words, the clinician can align them with the proper term—"obsession" or "compulsion"—for the family.

While introducing these concepts and their descriptive and operational boundaries, clinicians should try to gauge how helpful the child's report will be in arriving at symptom ratings. Some children are able to report quite reliably on their symptoms with parental help; some children are able to contribute to the discussion with parents providing most of the information; and some children because of immaturity, resistance, or both are not able to participate in the assessment, other than perhaps confirming or denying parents' impressions of symptoms.

Compulsions generally will be easier for the parents to observe and report upon, and it is more likely that children will be aware of their compulsions in comparison to thoughts/obsessions. Information about compulsions will also help anchor the child later when asking about obsessions. Clinicians can use the child's answers about compulsions as a starting point for questions about obsessions, for example, "You said that you wash your hands 3 times per hour, but you're not sure how often you worry about germs. Do you usually wash your hands when you're worrying about germs? Are there times that you worry about germs but don't wash your hands?"

If the child does not report obsessions, they may be inferred from parent report. However, the clinician should ensure that the parent thinks that anxiety may be driving the child's behavior. For example, a child may be washing his hands repeatedly but states that he does not worry about germs. Contamination obsessions may be inferred from the parent who reports that the child appears anxious while washing. Obsessions should not be inferred if the child does not seem anxious. In a case in which the child does not seem anxious (e.g., repeatedly lines up toys but does not seem bothered by it), the behavior may be self-stimulating or driven by another process, rather than a compulsion.

Family Considerations

When completing the initial evaluation of a young child with OCD, it is also important to consider that this may be a family's first contact with the mental health system. Parents of young children with OCD, by virtue of the fact that their children are young, are more likely to be experiencing their first contact as parents with the mental health system. They may be unfamiliar with the diagnostic process or ambivalent about obtaining treatment for their child. With a child of any age, disagreement with diagnosis and/or treatment approach can interfere with compliance. Parents of young children may be especially vulnerable to adherence difficulties. Thus, in the treatment of young children, it is especially important to identify and respond to issues of adjustment to having a child with a psychiatric problem.

Families are often unsure whether their child's symptoms are reflective of normative, if disturbing, developmental phases that the child will "outgrow," or whether they herald clinically serious issues. Moreover, entry into treatment is daunting for parents, who may be concerned that OCD symptoms at such a young age are perhaps insurmountable. Finally, given their child's developmental stage and the relatively greater demands that young children place on families, parents may have difficulty attending sessions, managing child oppositionality and treatment resistance, and consistently completing homework tasks. During the evaluation and the first two treatment sessions with parents alone, it is useful to address potential issues of the impact of treatment on the child and family, to problem solve around logistical obstacles in the scheduling of sessions and conducting homework tasks, and to provide a clear rationale for how and why treatment may work. Once the child has been properly evaluated and the clinician has laid the groundwork with the parents, treatment of the child can begin.

Chapter 3

Session 1: Introduction to the Treatment Program (Parents Only)

(Corresponds to chapter 1 of the workbook)

Materials Needed

- Assessment results

Outline

- Address process issues throughout session
- Establish rapport with parents or caretakers
- Assess overall impact of OCD and related behaviors on family functioning
- Provide psychoeducation about OCD as a neurobehavioral disorder
- Discuss the family's knowledge of OCD and cognitive-behavioral treatment (CBT)
- Explain the development and course of OCD
- Explain obsessive-compulsive spectrum disorders and comorbidity
- Differentiate between OCD behaviors and non-OCD behaviors
- Give overview of the treatment program
- Assign homework

Therapy Process Issues: Development of OCD

Much of this session relates to parents' feelings regarding the development of their child's OCD. Throughout the session, elicit from parents their thoughts or worries about why their child has OCD, where it has come from, etc. Differentiate an academic or medical understanding of OCD from other concerns the parents may have if this seems appropriate. The following questions may be helpful:

- *Parents often come to this treatment program with a number of thoughts or worries about why their child has OCD. What do you both think about this?*

- *Why do you think (child's name) has OCD?*

- *Do either of you feel guilty about this?*

- *Is anyone in the family getting blamed?*

Therapist Note

- *You may need to provide more examples or probes for some families. For example, some parents have told us that they think they have caused the OCD because of stress in the family, something they did wrong during pregnancy or early childhood, or their own anxiety.*

Establishing Rapport

Welcome the family to treatment. (*Note*: Before the first session, the patient should have already undergone full assessment and been diagnosed with early childhood–onset OCD). This session is designed only for parents. Given the child's young age, it is desirable to explain OCD to the parents alone and answer their questions, as well as gain an understanding of what the parents feel are the persistent problems relevant to the child's OCD. You may use the following dialogue to begin:

The purpose of today's session is to talk in some more detail about the ways in which (child's name)'s OCD is affecting everyone in the family. Specifically, we will talk about how you both may be involved in (child's name)'s symptoms and your views about how OCD developed. We want to talk about the diagnosis of OCD in young children and what treatments can help. We also want to discuss the difference between OCD and other anxieties or problem behaviors

that (child's name) might be having at home. Finally, we will give you
a more detailed overview of this treatment program and give you some
time to ask questions.

Assessment of Impact on Family Functioning

Therapist Note

░ *The elements in this section are required; however, the amount of time*
or depth devoted here is highly dependent on whether you were involved in
the initial assessment. If this is your first time with the family, this section
will take more time and attention. If you have completed the assessment
with the family, this section should be done as more of a quick review. ░

Troublesome Behaviors

First, distinguish which behaviors are related to OCD versus other problems. Prompt the parents by asking about OCD symptoms that were
reported during the initial assessment. Questions to ask include

░ *What does your child do that is causing the most concern at home*
or for the family?

░ *How does your child's (specific obsessions/compulsions) disrupt*
your family?

Family Involvement in OCD-Related Behaviors

Using examples specific to the child's symptoms, ascertain the nature
and degree of the family's involvement in the child's OCD behaviors.
You can review the results of the Family Accommodation and Impact
Scale-Child (FAIS-C) administered during the screening visit or re-
administer portions of the measure for clinical use. You may start with
the following dialogue:

During our last visit we reviewed the ways in which you may
reassure/engage in/tolerate/accommodate/modify your own routines in
response to (child's name)'s rituals. You identified _____ as major

areas of accommodation. Have you thought any more about these interactions? What are the results of your accommodations? What happens if the OCD behavior is not accommodated?

Discuss the impact of the child's behavior and parental accommodations on the family's overall functioning. Probe for specific impact of OCD behavior on and accommodation by other family members (e.g., siblings). Listen for themes related to short-term benefits of accommodation but long-term reinforcement of OCD behaviors.

Other Areas of Concern

Review any other areas of concern (anxiety or other behavioral problems) the child exhibits based on initial assessment results. Ask parents the following questions:

- *Do you have any other concerns at this time?*

- *How much trouble have these problems been causing for you and your family?*

OCD as a Neurobehavioral Disorder

This section begins the psychoeducation portion of the session. You may introduce it with the following dialogue:

This part of the session is intended to help you better understand OCD. I will be talking a little more than usual and going over a lot of information, but I am actually most interested in your thoughts and opinions. Feel free to ask questions and don't worry about remembering everything we talk about because a lot of this information will be covered in the workbook.

Reducing Blame

It is important to stress during this time that OCD is not the child's fault or the parents' fault. Providing information about what causes OCD helps illustrate the point that the child or family is not to blame.

Comparing OCD to a "medical illness" sometimes helps clarify this point. You may use the following dialogue:

OCD is a biological disorder. It is not your child's fault, or yours, that he has OCD. There is nothing that you or your child has "done" to make him have OCD. How would it feel different if your child were diagnosed with diabetes or another chronic medical condition?

Medical Understanding

Ask parents to provide their own thoughts about how children develop OCD. Tell parents that you will continue to talk about these ideas or worries throughout the treatment program. For now, though, you will review some information about our medical understanding of OCD.

Therapist Note

▓ *You will need to tailor the next section to some extent based on the parents' current working model of how their child developed the disorder.* ▓

Discuss differences in brain structure and function and the link between serotonin and OCD. Explain that one way to think of OCD is that the "wiring" in the child's brain is different from that of a child without OCD. People with OCD receive messages differently than people without OCD because of the difference in brain "wiring." Researchers have found that serotonin, one of the chemicals in the brain that sends messages to other parts of the brain, is linked to OCD. Medications that work on serotonin can be used to manage OCD symptoms, but their safety and effectiveness with young children have yet to be fully established. However, these biological differences have been shown to respond to behavioral treatments; this program uses a behavioral approach to safely and effectively treat a child's OCD.

Also note that genetic factors may contribute to the development of OCD. Research shows that OCD runs in families, especially those of young children with OCD.

Therapist Note

▨ Tailor the following section to families based on assessment of family knowledge about OCD. ▨

Defining Obsessions and Compulsions

Ask parents to provide their definitions of obsessions and compulsions. Clarify using the following definitions.

▨ *Obsessions* are persistent impulses, ideas, images, or thoughts that intrude into a person's thinking and cause excessive worry and anxiety.

▨ *Compulsions* are mental acts or repetitive behaviors performed in response to obsessions to relieve or prevent worry and/or anxiety.

Illustrate these definitions by giving an example of the child's obsessions and compulsions:

For example, (child's name) does this (give presenting behavior) to relieve this (give presenting obsession). Doing this helps him feel less anxious and more "in control" of the intrusive thought.

Explain that obsessions and compulsions are most commonly related to some general categories (fear of harm coming to self or others, fear of illness, washing, hoarding, ordering, etc.) but can be very different depending on the child and are often different in younger children.

Understanding the Diagnosis of OCD

Next, ask parents to provide their own definition or understanding of the diagnosis of OCD. Clarify using the following information. To be diagnosed with OCD, a person can have obsessions and/or compulsions. It is not uncommon for young children to report only compulsions (rituals). Additionally, the symptoms must take up at least 1 hr per day and cause significant interference in daily life (e.g., get in the way of functioning at home or at school). The rituals/obsessions cannot be developmentally appropriate or expected (to be discussed later).

Understanding Cognitive-Behavioral Treatment

Ask parents to provide their own definition or understanding of CBT and exposure with response prevention (E/RP). Clarify using the following information. CBT is a special type of psychotherapy that—just like the name suggests—focuses on thoughts and behaviors. The specific kind of CBT for OCD is called E/RP and in this case is focused on treating the whole family as well as the child. The theory behind E/RP is that in order to treat OCD successfully, we need to reduce obsessions or feelings of discomfort that lead to rituals. An effective way to do this is to slowly expose the child to the situations that are most uncomfortable until the child feels less fearful (this is called habituation).

Stress that this type of treatment is challenging for anyone, but young children in particular need a great deal of support and help from their parents in order to be successful.

Development and Course of OCD

Prevalence

Discuss the prevalence of OCD with the parents. You may use the following dialogue:

> *Do you have any guess about how common OCD is in children? We think that about one or two kids out of every hundred have OCD. That's a lot of people. In a school of 1000 kids that means maybe 10–20 kids have OCD.*

Onset

Explain how OCD develops and relate it to the child's case. Ask parents whether they remember when they first noticed the child's OCD symptoms. Tell them that OCD typically has a gradual onset. They may have noticed the child becoming more rigid about certain things. The child probably started to become more upset when a ritual was disrupted or more "worried" by obsessive thoughts.

Some cases of OCD appear following a stressful life event or a medical illness, and the symptoms have a more rapid onset. For example, recent research shows that OCD symptoms may appear following strep throat. Discuss pediatric autoimmune neuropsychiatric disorders associated with streptococcal infections (PANDAS) in more detail, if applicable.

Obsessive-Compulsive Spectrum Disorders and Comorbidity

You may begin this discussion by asking parents whether they knew that OCD often occurs along with other disorders. Inform the parents that in some cases of OCD, other psychiatric disorders are present which can also complicate the diagnosis of OCD. Tic disorders, anxiety disorders, behavior problems, and learning disorders are especially common in young children with OCD. If relevant to the specific child, you may need to discuss this further. The purpose of this discussion would be to begin to differentiate for the parents which particular symptoms will be the focus of treatment, and conversely, which will not be directly addressed.

OCD Versus Non-OCD Behaviors

Differentiate between OCD behaviors and non-OCD behaviors, such as developmentally appropriate rituals or obsessions and oppositional behaviors. Tell parents that throughout this program, you will be discussing the difference between the following:

- Rituals or obsessions that are common to most kids

- Rituals or obsessions that are excessive and indicative of OCD

- Non-OCD related behaviors (e.g., other anxiety disorders, normal child misbehavior, and aggressive or oppositional behaviors)

Ask parents the following questions:

- *Have you thought about the differences between these types of behaviors in the past few weeks?*

- *Do you think it is clear which behaviors are related to OCD?*

Stress to parents that telling the difference between these behaviors is not an easy task. Remind them that most children exhibit ritualistic or superstitious behaviors at some point during development, and these behaviors are sometimes exacerbated at times of transition or stress (e.g., starting school or birth of a sibling).

Normal Developmental Rituals

Review normal developmental rituals at different ages. Provide parents with information about behavior that is typical for different developmental ages (adapted from Francis & Gragg, 1996):

- Around age 2, children are often very rigid about eating, bathing, and bedtime routines.

- Between ages 3 and 5, children often repeat the same activity again and again during play (e.g., building a tower and knocking it down).

- From ages 5 to 6, children are often very attuned to rules associated with games and may become distressed if these rules are changed.

- Children between the ages of 6 and 11 often engage in superstitious behavior to prevent bad things from happening, and they may show increased interest in keeping a collection of objects (e.g., baseball cards).

- At age 12 and older, children may be very absorbed in particular activities (e.g., video games) or with particular people (e.g., movie stars); they may also show superstitious behavior in relation to making good things happen (e.g., performance in sports).

Emphasize to parents that it is important to determine that the child's ritualistic behavior is different from that of other children his age.

Children with OCD are more rigid about rituals than children who do not have OCD. Young children with OCD become very upset if a ritual is disrupted, whereas children without OCD are not as greatly affected by disruptions to routines. Children with OCD also feel anxious if they are prevented from completing a ritual and are more difficult to distract from a ritual or an obsessive thought. OCD rituals are often more elaborate or dramatic than the rituals of children the same age who do not have OCD.

Other Kinds of Anxieties and Misbehavior

It is also important to recognize that OCD is different from other kinds of anxieties that the child may have (e.g., SAD, GAD, or phobia). Ask parents whether they can think of any examples of other kinds of anxieties specific to their child.

In addition, it is often confusing for parents to separate OCD symptoms from other kinds of misbehavior. Ask parents whether they can think of examples of their child's behavior that might be confused with OCD. Also ask them whether they can think of examples of acting out or oppositional behavior that are clearly different than OCD.

Overview of the Treatment Program

The goals of this section are the following:

- To introduce the parenting "tools" concept

- To discuss philosophy of parent or family involvement in treatment

You may use the following dialogue to transition to this portion of the session:

We have spent a good deal of time today talking about the specifics of OCD and how it affects everyone in the family. I actually want to switch gears a little now and talk some more about what this treatment program is going to involve over the next few months.

Parent "Tools"

Explain that, as parents might imagine, treating OCD in young children is very different than treating OCD in adolescents or adults or even older children. This cognitive-behavioral family treatment focuses on the ways to decrease OCD symptoms, but because the child is so young, much of the treatment program is focused on helping parents find the tools they need to help their children. Families will learn and practice specific techniques that other families have found helpful in dealing with similar kinds of problems. These include techniques for both parents and children to use.

Family Involvement

In addition to talking about and practicing these specific techniques or tools, parents and children come together during sessions to discuss issues of importance to the family. Besides reducing the child's OCD symptoms, the specific goals are the following:

- To promote positive family problem solving related to OCD (e.g., reduce family accommodation of OCD symptoms and reduce criticism or hostility related to OCD)

- To help parents to understand how their own fears and anxieties interact with the child's behavior

Stress that we believe this type of family collaboration is essential for successful implementation of OCD treatment in this age group.

Wrap-Up

Ask parents whether they have any questions about the material covered in today's session. You may end with the following dialogue.

The materials we have covered today are a good introduction to the kinds of things we will be talking about over the course of the next 12 sessions. As we have said, because your child is so young, much of our treatment program is focused on teaching you the tools you need to help your child.

Tell parents that it is expected that all primary caretakers will attend all scheduled sessions and that they will complete homework assignments with the child. Try to problem solve with parents any issues with attendance, homework, etc.

Homework

 ✎ Have parents make a daily list of all OCD behaviors and record the amount of time the child spent engaging in each behavior on the Session 1 homework sheet provided in the workbook.

Chapter 4   *Session 2: Laying the Groundwork (Parents Only)*

(Corresponds to chapter 2 of the workbook)

Materials Needed

- Daily Record of OCD Symptoms
- Hierarchy Form 1
- Reward Chart

Outline

- Address process issues throughout the session
- Review past week with parents
- Initiate development of OCD symptom hierarchy
- Give overview of child and parent tools for treatment
- Introduce differential attention
- Introduce reward plan
- Assign homework

Therapy Process Issues: Identifying and Addressing Misperceptions

This session's process issues are to identify negative or distorted assumptions and attitudes about OCD and/or the child and help the family to correct these misperceptions. Address negative and incorrect attributions or assumptions throughout the session as appropriate. Also, discuss the family's expectations for treatment and whether these expectations are realistic. Asking parents the following questions may be helpful:

- *You probably remember that we spent some time last week talking about your thoughts or worries about how (child's name) developed OCD. Have you thought more about this?*

- *Based on our discussion last week, how much do you feel you child can control her OCD symptoms and behaviors?*

- *What kinds of things seem to affect (child's name)'s ability to control OCD?*

- *How do you usually react to (child's name)'s OCD? Do the two of you have different reactions? What kinds of things seem to change your reactions?*

- *How do (child's name)'s siblings respond to her OCD? What is their understanding of OCD? Does OCD cause conflict between siblings at home?*

Continue to emphasize the idea that parents and siblings should not blame the child for having OCD. Explore family members' feelings about OCD and attributions or negative distortions the family may have about the child. You may ask parents whether they would feel or act differently if their child were diagnosed with an illness other than OCD. Compare reactions to physical versus mental illness and OCD versus other mental illness. Discuss what would be different and why. The emotions to listen for include helplessness, frustration, resentment, jealousy, disappointment, and embarrassment. The function of this discussion is to help parents express these feelings in their own words and for the therapist to be empathic about the parents' experience. The following cues may be helpful in eliciting parent discussion about their emotions.

- *How do you feel when (child's name) is struggling with OCD?*

- *What do you feel like it means about you as a parent when your child is struggling with OCD?*

Answer any questions that have arisen since the previous session. Ascertain which OCD symptoms have caused problems during the past week; this will help to lay the groundwork for hierarchy development later in the session. This discussion can be used to draw out "process" themes listed in the previous section. Try to help parents come up with some of these points on their own. Also review the homework and problem solve any obstacles to completion. You may ask the following questions:

- *Do you have any questions from our last session?*

- *How was this past week? Were there any significant events?*

- *Generally speaking, what were the major concerns this past week?*

- *Were there any problems with the homework?*

Initial Development of OCD Symptom Hierarchy

After reviewing the homework from last week, evaluate which symptoms are directly related to OCD and which belong to other areas (e.g., other anxiety or behavior problems) that are not the current focus of treatment. You may start the discussion by reviewing the child's primary OCD symptoms at this point. Ask parents whether there is anything that is not represented on their homework from this past week.

Therapist Note

- *Make sure that parents understand the difference between OCD symptoms and other concerns, and that you are in agreement with the parents about the targets of treatment.*

Determine also which OCD behaviors are the most troublesome. The family should rank OCD symptoms from least to most bothersome. Record these on the Hierarchy Form 1 provided in this chapter; you may photocopy this form as needed. See also Figure 4.1 for an example of a completed hierarchy. At this point, it is fine to either get a lot of detail about a small number of symptoms or discuss many symptoms

Ranking	Description of Symptom	Label (O, C, ?)	Notes
1.	Worries about household cleaners	O	
2.	Avoiding eating off recently cleaned surfaces	C	
3.	Questioning parents about use of household cleaners	C	
4.	Worries about mold on food	O	
5.	Examination of food for mold	C	
6.	Worries about whether she had swallowed objects (e.g., paper clip)	O	
7.	Avoiding eating certain foods	?	Need more info

Figure 4.1

Example of Completed Hierarchy Form 1

Hierarchy Form 1

Ranking	Description of Symptom	Label (O, C, ?)	Notes

Instructions: Please keep a *daily* record of **TWO** of your child's OCD symptoms. In the space provided below (feel free to use additional space if necessary) record the date, the specific symptom, the amount of time your child spent engaging in that symptom, how much disturbance it causes in the family, and how the parents are involved in the symptom.

Date	OCD symptom	Time spent	Family disturbance	Parent's involvement
T 3/17	At dinner, looked at roll for mold	5 min	Made us run late for basketball	Answered many questions
W 3/18	Refused to eat muffin for breakfast	10 min	Fought on way to school	Yelled at her
W 3/18	Asked if she would get sick from Lysol	1 min	None	Told her not to worry (2x)
Th 3/19	Looked at bagel for mold	4 min	None	Answered many questions
F 3/20	Asked about bottle of Windex	1 min	None	Told her not to worry (2x)
Sa 3/21	Looked at dinner roll for mold	1 min	She cried	Answered many questions
Su 3/22	Asked if she would get sick from Windex	1 min	None	Told her not to worry
M 3/23	Refused to eat toast	5 min	Late to school b/c made eggs	Answered many questions

Figure 4.2

Example of Completed Daily Record of OCD Symptoms

in less detail. These symptoms will be used in the following session to create a behavior chart and exposure plan. You may use the following dialogue:

> *Now that we have a list, let's try and put them in order from the easiest to work on to the hardest. This list will change once we get more input from (child's name) in the next session. It will also continue to change throughout treatment as we get more information and your child progresses.*

Explain that for this week, parents are going to pick two symptoms and record some more specific information. Refer parents to the Session 2 homework sheet in the workbook. See Figure 4.2 for a completed example of the form. For homework, parents are to record the following:

- How much time each behavior absorbs

- How much disturbance each behavior causes in the family

- How much the parents are involved in the symptoms

Overview of Parent and Child Tools for Treatment

The goal of this section is to introduce and briefly discuss each of the child and parent tools that will be used in treatment. You may use the following dialogue to begin:

> *We talked last week about how part of our program involves teaching both you and your child the tools to reduce the severity of OCD. Today we are going to do a quick review of all the parent tools and child tools your family will be learning in treatment. Then, we will talk some more about and practice one of these parent tools. Before we start, there are a few things to know. You are probably familiar with the kinds of ideas we will talk about today—just like you might have many tools in your toolbox at home with a basic idea of how they work (some more than others). The interesting thing about tools, though, is that some tools can be used in many different ways, and sometimes one tool is more effective than another for a certain task. In other words, you already know how to use a hammer, but we want you to use it like a carpenter.*

Explain to parents that the goal is to work together to make the best use of these parenting "tools" in the group effort to reduce the impact of OCD on the family. Over the course of treatment, parents will discuss all of these tools in more detail with you, practice them in session, and practice them at home with their child. Today's session begins with an overview of the tools, so that parents know where they are headed in the coming weeks.

Tools for the Child

Inform parents that in this treatment program, their child will practice

- Identifying and monitoring OCD symptoms

- Learning how to externalize ("boss back") OCD

- Using a feelings thermometer to rate anxiety

- Working with parents to develop a hierarchy and implement E/RP

Tools for the Parents

Parents learn along with their children and encourage and support practice outside of sessions. General parenting tools emphasized throughout treatment include the following:

- *Differential attention:* using attention to change a child's behavior

- *Modeling:* becoming aware of how parent behavior influences child behavior

- *Scaffolding:* working alongside a child to change her emotional response to a certain event or situation and ultimately help her to respond in more adaptive and independent ways

Differential Attention (1): Tangible Rewards

The first parenting tool to be discussed is differential attention. You may begin with the following dialogue:

One of the tools we just talked about is something we call differential attention—as we said earlier, the basic idea is that you can use your attention to change your child's behaviors. That is, you will give attention to the behaviors you want to see and withhold attention from the behaviors you don't want to see. Another way to think about this is that when you reward a behavior, it increases in frequency and when you don't reward it, it decreases.

Background Information on Child Behavior

Start the discussion with some background information about child behavior in general (the following is adapted from Stark, 2003). A basic way that children learn to act is by learning what happens after they act in a certain way (e.g., how their parents respond). They then learn to act in ways that lead to the results they want. One of the results children most want is *adult attention*. As parents know, children often do all sorts of things (both positive and negative) to get adult attention. The interesting thing about this is that for many children adult attention is a reward regardless of whether it is positive (e.g., saying "good job") or negative (saying "I told you to stop doing that!"). While adults do not tend to think of a scolding being very rewarding, it still provides attention to the child. The problem is that in the midst of a busy day adults are much more likely to notice and comment on "bad" behavior because it interferes with the other things they are trying to do. In addition, adults often do not actively comment on or respond to the "good" behavior because they perceive it as what the child "is supposed to be doing." Therefore, children will often behave in ways their parents do not like because it gives them immediate attention, at least for a little while.

Positive Reinforcement

Ask parents what are some ways that they give their child positive reinforcement. Discuss in what circumstances it is the easiest for them to give positive reinforcers and when it is harder to do this.

Explain that there are different kinds of positive reinforcers:

1. tangible rewards such as giving a child a piece of candy or a small toy

2. privileges such as allowing a child extra computer time or a later bedtime

3. praise and encouragement such as saying "great job" or giving a child a hug (positive attention)

Tell parents that today's session focuses on tangible rewards and granting privileges. Next week's session covers positive attention, such as verbal and physical praise. The following session then moves on to talking about the flip side of this tool—removal of attention from certain behaviors (the idea being that taking attention away from a behavior or not rewarding it will decrease its frequency). These tools will increase the likelihood that the child will practice the skills she will be learning in therapy. Specifically, parents will give their child positive reinforcers (such as rewards) for practicing the therapy skills. You may use the following dialogue:

> *As I said earlier about tools in a toolbox, I am sure that you are familiar with using positive reinforcement as a tool to increase the desirable things that (child's name) does. We are going to focus on using this tool as part of a structured plan to increase your child's motivation for treatment. Today we are going to discuss using tangible rewards, because we feel it is important to review using a reward program with you before (child's name) comes in next week. As I said earlier, we will continue to talk about positive reinforcement, specifically praise and encouragement, next week.*

Introduction to Reward Plan

The goals of this section are to explain the rationale and implementation of a reward plan, and how it differs from bribery. Tell parents that the reward plan is one of the ways that we put parenting tools into action in this treatment. Rewards are a form of positive reinforcement that is very effective in increasing behaviors we want to see more of. Emphasize that all of us need rewards to do things that are challenging (e.g., most of us would not go to work everyday unless we received a paycheck). Ask parents the following questions:

- *Can you think of some ways that you or others reward your child for doing things that are hard?*
- *What do you think about using rewards in general?*
- *What do you think about using rewards to get kids to do things?*
- *Is there anything about rewards that you would like to discuss before we talk about the details of the reward plan?*
- *Have you ever tried using a reward plan before with (child's name)? If so, how did it work?*

Some parents have tried using rewards with their child and been disappointed with the results. Tell parents that we find that including a reward program as part of our treatment really can help children in their efforts. A reward plan will be an important motivator to help the child face OCD. There are different types of rewards that can be used, and you and the parents will decide together on some appropriate ones for their family. In fact, some of the things parents do already may have a reward component to them without parents even being aware of it.

Therapist Note

Tailor the next part of this discussion to the family. For example, address problems they may have had with rewards in the past (e.g., picking too many goals, feeling like it was bribery, or using rewards that were too big or expensive).

Rewards Versus Bribery

When we talk about positive rewards, sometimes parents think it sounds like bribing a child to behave. Stress that rewards are actually very different from bribery. The major difference is that these types of rewards are planned and proactive. Rewards are connected to specific behaviors, both of which have been determined ahead of time. The rewards are set up beforehand to help a child stay motivated to control her behavior and to make good behavioral choices. This is very different than offering rewards out of desperation (e.g., a child having a tantrum in a toy store is given a toy to quiet down; a child who won't stop a compulsion is told if she gets in the car now she will get something she really wants). In these situations, rewards are being used to get quick control of a child who is misbehaving or having great difficulty with an anxiety-provoking situation. With our plan, parents will reward a child for practicing therapy skills and facing her fears—appropriate behaviors they might reward anyway.

Key Components of Successful Reward Programs

Summarize the key components of successful reward programs:

1. The plan should be simple and easy to follow—ideally targeting specific, easy to observe behaviors.

2. Rewards should be delivered promptly following desired behaviors.

3. Rewards should be frequent enough that the child will be encouraged to work toward them.

4. Rewards should be something the child enjoys and that the parents are going to feel okay about if the child does not get it (e.g., stickers, playing a game, spending time with someone special, food, or a small toy).

5. Rewards have to be delivered consistently.

Situations in Which to Reward the Child

There are several different situations in which it is appropriate to reward the child. Review these with parents.

Completing Homework

At the end of each session, you will be assigning "homework" to the child. These assignments will be exercises that she should be working on at home to help her keep track of OCD symptoms or practice "bossing back" OCD. The treatment reward plan uses daily rewards at home for completing homework tasks. Explain that because you will all be working at the child's pace and the child will have control over items being worked on, with parents' guidance the child should be successful with practicing the chosen items. At the beginning, these tasks will be short, and parents should give rewards for every step toward positive progress.

On-Task Behavior

Rewards can also be used in and between sessions to encourage the child to do the things required for learning new skills (e.g., listening and following directions) or to actually "boss back" OCD. If necessary, you and parents can work together to devise a plan to target behaviors that help the child stay on task as they become apparent during and between sessions.

Specific Rewards

Explain to parents that we often use stickers as small rewards that can be delivered immediately after the child does something positive and then these small rewards can be cashed in for larger rewards at certain intervals. For example, parents will give their child a sticker each day of the week that she completes an assigned task. The child will then receive a weekly reward in-session for earning a certain number of stickers at home during the week (all rewards for the week will be decided in the previous session). Sometimes, stickers are not enough to motivate the child to practice at home, so discuss with the parents other rewards that could be used with their child. Ask them what they consider appropriate and inappropriate for rewards.

Developing a Reward Chart

Refer parents to the example reward chart included in this chapter (also provided in the workbook). In the next session, they will decide what kind of reward chart will work for their family. Guide the parents to think about the following areas, which are the ones that require the most adaptation to the child's developmental level:

1. How often should the child be eligible to receive a reward and will the parent be able to reliably deliver (e.g., once a day may be fine for older children; several times a day is preferable for younger children, such as before breakfast, before lunch, before dinner, and after dinner)

2. What kind of reward(s) will the family use (e.g., small tokens delivered more frequently combined with bigger reinforcers delivered less often)

3. What behaviors will be rewarded; specifically, how big a string of behaviors will the child have to perform to earn the reward (e.g., one behavior is advisable for younger children and multistep behavior chains are possible for older children in the 5–8 age range)

Homework

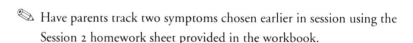

 ✎ Have parents track two symptoms chosen earlier in session using the Session 2 homework sheet provided in the workbook.

✎ Ask parents to think about and be prepared to discuss the following with their child in session next week: (1) examples of specific rewards that will motivate their child and (2) an example of a reward chart that may work for them at home.

REWARD CHART

Week of _____

Homework	Mon	Tue	Wed	Thu	Fri	Sat	Sun

Chapter 5

Session 3: Child Introduction to the Treatment Program

(Corresponds to chapters 2 and 3 of the workbook)

Materials Needed

- Hierarchy Form 2
- Hierarchy Form 3
- Feelings Thermometer
- Monitoring Form
- Reward Chart

Outline

- Establish rapport with child
- Review past week
- Introduce child to treatment program
- Introduce child to reward program
- Review OCD symptoms with child
- Introduce feelings thermometer and symptom tracking (child tools)
- Discuss differential attention, specifically praise and encouragement (parent tools)
- Review level of family involvement in OCD symptoms
- Assign homework
- Create a new hierarchy between sessions (therapist only)

Therapist Note

As there is a fair amount of content to cover, there are no specific process issues to address this session.

Establishing Rapport With the Child

The approach to the development of rapport with the child in this section will depend on many factors: whether you did the initial assessment with the child, the child's age, and the child's anxiety level. This may not happen at the start of the session as it may be easier for the child to "settle in" before having to answer questions or take a significant role in the session.

Welcome to Treatment

Introduce the purpose of treatment. The nature of this discussion will depend on the age of the child. Older children will be able to have more detailed conversations about their OCD symptoms and may also benefit from some individual time with you. If you and the child have not met before, it makes sense to start by asking more general questions about the child's life, school, interests, etc. You may start with something similar to the following sample dialogue:

What did mom and dad tell you about why you are here today? Just like when you were here before (for the assessment) we are going to talk about your OCD (use the term that the child or family uses if possible). We are also going to be talking about other stuff that kids have problems with. For the next few months, I will work with you and your parents to help make it so that OCD does not cause so many problems for you.

Normalizing the Experience

Emphasize that it is not the child's or his parents' fault that he has OCD. You can tell the child that there is nothing that he or his parents have "done" to make him have OCD. Also, normalize the disorder as with the following dialogue:

> *Lots of kids come to treatment feeling like they are the only ones to have OCD or that something is wrong with them. Actually, there are lots and lots of kids who have OCD. There are probably a couple of kids in your school who also think they are the only ones with OCD. What do you think about that?*

Review of Past Week

Review the previous session with parents. Answer any questions that have arisen in the past week. Ascertain which OCD behaviors have caused problems during the past week to lay the groundwork for hierarchy development later in the session. Homework will be reviewed and discussed in more detail later in the session. You may ask the following questions:

- *Do you have any questions from our last session?*

- *How was this past week? Were there any significant events?*

- *Can everyone identify something good that has happened in the past week?*

- *How did the homework go?*

Introduction of Treatment Program to Child

Therapist Note

The amount of detail given will depend on the age and anxiety level of the child as well as on any prior relationship with the therapist (during the assessment).

Naming the Child's OCD

First, create a name for the child's OCD. This portion will be largely dependent on the age of the child. Older children will be able to more easily grasp the concept of OCD and thus will probably have an easier time coming up with a "nasty name" (March & Mulle, 1998) for OCD. Some children may have a name they call it already (e.g., worries, questions, or habits), and it might be helpful to refer to OCD the way the child or family refers to it. This name should be used throughout the sessions. If developmentally appropriate, talk about the difference between obsessions and compulsions, making specific connections to the child's symptoms.

What the Program Involves

Give the child a general description of the treatment program. You may use the following dialogue:

> *You, your parents, and I will all be working together to decrease your worries (or use child's word) by fighting back against them and proving that you are the boss. It is kind of like we are all on a team fighting against OCD. This probably sounds hard and it might seem scary. It is important that you know that we will work on easier things first and will work at your pace. Our only goal is that we are always making some progress.*

Depending on the age of the child, you can provide psychoeducation about OCD as a neurobiological illness at this point. Emphasize that many other kids have the same kinds of worries and behaviors and have gotten better by fighting back against them.

Introduction to the Reward Program

Next, introduce the child to the reward program. You may want to use the following dialogue:

> *We are going to be working on lots of things with you and your mom and dad. Sometimes this can be hard work, but we all think you can do this. And when you work hard you will be able to get rewards for doing a great job!*

Brainstorming Ideas for Rewards

Brainstorm ideas for rewards (e.g., stickers, special meals, and family outings) with the child and family. Have parents share the ideas that they came up with. Ask the child the following questions:

- *What are some rewards or prizes that you can think of?*

- *We had your mom and dad think of some things last week too—did they share these with you? What do you think of their ideas?*

Make sure to include parents in the brainstorming session and come up with reasonable ideas that the family will be able to carry out.

How to Use Rewards

Explain that each week the child will have different things to work on after he goes home from session. The parents will keep track of how he does and give him a chance to earn rewards. The child will earn daily rewards at home for doing his assignments. If he does his homework a certain number of days (to be decided on together), then he can earn another reward when he comes to therapy.

Note: Another option is to use rewards provided weekly by the therapist as a motivator for the child to actively participate in session (e.g., perform in-session exposure) later in treatment.

Pick with the family rewards for daily, weekly, and in-session (if appropriate) completion of assignments. You, the parents, and the child should all be in agreement on the reward terms.

Review of OCD Symptoms

Review the OCD symptom hierarchy developed with parents in the last session. The goal is to have child contribute to the development of the hierarchy as much as possible. Some children may be able to add or modify the existing hierarchy. Younger children may only listen to items on the list developed by parents and help to provide ratings later in the session.

Figure out the child's language for talking about his OCD symptoms. Does the child see his OCD as a problem? Make sure the child knows what symptoms you have been discussing with his parents. See the following sample dialogues:

> *Last time you were here we talked about a lot of worries. You told me that _____ worries you and/or you do _____ a lot. Have you noticed any other worries/things that you do over and over again?*

> *Your parents have said that ___ causes you problems at home. (Review parent hierarchy developed in last session and look at homework.) What do you think about this list? Do you think anything is missing?*

Introduction to Feelings Thermometer and Self-Monitoring

Have the child use the feelings thermometer in the workbook to give anxiety ratings to OCD items (if possible). Have the child participate in reordering the OCD symptom hierarchy using the Hierarchy Form 2 provided in this chapter (you may photocopy this form as needed).

Therapist Note

▨ *Since the OCD behaviors of young children are embedded in the family structure, and because young children are not cognitively able to externalize the OCD as well as older children, the level of parental involvement in this section should be tailored to meet the needs of the family. Parents are usually in tune with which "worries" are the most troublesome to their child.* ▨

Feelings Thermometer

A feelings thermometer is used to measure the child's level of anxiety regarding specific situations. The feelings thermometer is also useful for E/RP tasks. Using the list of OCD behaviors just generated, get ratings of each item if possible (the extent to which this is possible in session will depend on many factors—time spent developing hierarchy, child's understanding of the thermometer ratings, etc.). Parents will play a crucial role in helping most children to make ratings. In the case of some younger children, parents may need to make the ratings without significant input from the child.

You may want to use the following dialogue to introduce the feelings thermometer (Figure 5.1):

> *Do you know what a thermometer is? What are some things that we use thermometers for? That's right, we use them to measure temperature, which helps us figure things out, like whether you have a fever and need to take medicine, or how cold it is outside and whether we need to wear a coat. A feelings thermometer is just like other thermometers only it measures feelings instead of temperature. Knowing how you feel or how much you feel something will help us work together in this treatment. Here is a picture of a feelings thermometer. At the top of the picture next to the frowning face is the number 10. If you rated something with a frowning face and a 10, that would mean that you felt really bad or anxious about the situation you were rating. At the bottom of the picture is a smiling face and the number 0. If you rated something with a smiling face and a 0 that would mean that you didn't feel anxious or bad about the situation you were rating. Imagine that in the middle is a picture with neither a smile nor a frown and the number 5. What should we call this kind of face? (If child doesn't offer an option, suggest calling it medium face.) This means that you feel some anxiety or bad feelings about the situation you are rating. Can you give me some examples of things that you would rate with a smiley face? a medium face? and a frowning face? We will use the feelings thermometer to rate your OCD symptoms from the least upsetting to the most upsetting.*

The feelings thermometer may need to be made simpler (e.g., ignoring 0–10 scale) and/or may require use of another metaphor to facilitate its use with younger kids. Two metaphors that we have found helpful are depicted in the alternative feelings rating scales provided in this chapter (see Figures 5.2 and 5.3). One uses the metaphor of carrying heavy bricks; the number of bricks corresponds to the load that the child is bearing in a particular situation. The other uses the metaphor of butterflies in the tummy; the number of butterflies corresponds to the level of the child's distress. The standard feelings thermometer is

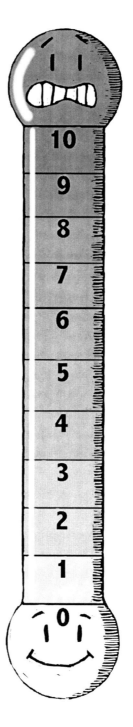

Figure 5.1
Feelings Thermometer

Figure 5.2

Bricks Feelings Thermometer

included in the child tools in Chapter 3 of the workbook; a My Feelings Thermometer page is also provided for the child to create his own version (e.g., using a metaphor).

Therefore, the content in the "Ratings" column of the hierarchy form will vary according to the developmental level of the child (e.g., numbers, faces, or high/medium/low). See Figure 5.4 for an example of a completed hierarchy with ratings. A blank Hierarchy Form 2 is also included in this chapter; you may photocopy this form as needed. The hierarchy created using the feelings thermometer in this session should be modified throughout the subsequent sessions, with new symptoms added and old symptoms reevaluated as needed.

Self-Monitoring

The goal is to have the family monitor one to two OCD symptoms every day. The child should have a specific monitoring task which will

Figure 5.3

Butterflies Feelings Thermometer

Ranking	Description of Symptom	Label (O, C, ?)	Rating	Notes
1.	Worries about household cleaners (e.g., Windex)	O	☹	If he smells it or sees the bottle these are triggers
2.	Avoiding eating off recently cleaned surfaces	C	☹	Seeing shiny or wet surfaces in the kitchen
3.	Questioning parents about use of household cleaners	C	☹	
4.	Worries about mold on food	O	☹	
5.	Examination of food for mold (self)	C	☹	
6.	Asking family member to examine food for mold	C	☹	
7.	Avoiding eating food that is likely to be moldy (e.g., bread, muffins)	C	☹	
8.	Worries about whether he had swallowed objects (e.g., paper clip)	O	☹	
9.	Worries about touching dirt on the floor	O	☺	

Figure 5.4

Example of Completed Hierarchy Form 2

Hierarchy Form 2

Ranking	Description of Symptom	Label	Rating	Notes

differ depending on the child's age, cognitive level, etc. You should be flexible, but ideas include the following:

- Child marks chart independently
- Child tells a parent each time he engages in a symptom so parent can mark the chart
- Child cooperates in talking with parents when they ask about the specific symptoms at an agreed upon time each day

Work with child and family to develop a plan or chart that makes sense for them. For examples, see Figure 5.5 of a completed Monitoring Form and Figure 5.6 of a completed Reward Chart that tracks child participation in the monitoring process. Blank copies of both the Monitoring Form and Reward Chart are provided in the workbook. It is fine to emphasize breadth (track multiple symptoms) or depth (track one symptom with more detail). Depending on the child's age and developmental level, parents may or may not play an active role in monitoring. It is important that the family practice something out of session related to talking about or keeping track of OCD.

Have the family pick one or two symptoms to keep track of how often they happen each day during the next week. (*Note*: it makes sense to choose items that you are likely to target as initial E/RP tasks). Go over what the child's task will be and the parents' role in monitoring. See the following sample dialogues:

> **For Child:** *We will use this chart and have you make a mark on the chart (or agreed-upon system) each time you do (symptom name). You can earn rewards for completing the chart. For example, you can earn a sticker for the day on your sticker chart for keeping track of (symptom name). Does this make sense to everyone? Next week, we will start to think about "bossing around" OCD, but this week we will just keep track of it.*

> **For Parents:** *When you do help (child's name) with or notice an OCD behavior you can label the request/behavior as related to OCD in a non-critical way. Saying something like "Do you think this is part of OCD? This will be a good thing to talk about when we go see (name of child's therapist) next week." The goal is to set the stage for your child to be able to identify and report on some of his symptoms, which we will begin to work on in the next session.*

Instructions: Please keep a *daily* record of **TWO** of your child's OCD symptoms. In the space provided below (feel free to use additional space if necessary) record the date, the specific symptom, the amount of time your child spent engaging in that symptom, and how parents are involved in the symptom. Try to involve your child in some aspect of monitoring and recording symptoms. Reward child for participation in this process.

Date	OCD symptom	Time spent	Parent's involvement	Child involved in monitoring/recording (Y/N)
T 3/24	Worried about Lysol in bathroom	10 min	Answered questions; then got angry	Y
W 3/25	Refused to eat bagel	10 min	Yelled at him	N
W 3/25	Worried about Windex	1 min	Answered questions	Y
W 3/25	Refused to eat dinner roll	1 min	Reassured not moldy	Y
Th 3/26	Worried about Lysol in bathroom	2 min	Answered questions	Y
Th 3/26	Inspected toast for mold	1 min	Ignored	Y
Th 3/26	Worried about Windex	5 min	Answered questions	Y
Th 3/26	Worried about swallowing paper clip	5 min	Reassured	Y
Th 3/26	Checked roll for mold	1 min	Ignored	Y
Th 3/26	Worried about Lysol in bathroom	5 min	Reassured	Y
F 3/27	Worried about Lysol in bathroom	1 min	Ignored	Y
F 3/27	Worried about swallowing Windex	10 min	Reassured	Y
F 3/27	Worried about chemical smell	10 min	Reassured	Y
Su 3/29	Checked roll for mold	1 min	Answered questions	Y

Figure 5.5

Example of Completed Monitoring Form

Homework	Mon	Tue	Wed	Thurs	Fri	Sat	Sun
Tell parent when OCD happens (reward for each instance)	Before school ★ ★	Before school ★	Before school	Before school ★ ★	Before school	Before lunch	Before lunch
Tell parent when OCD happens (reward for each instance)	After school ★	After school	After school ★ ★	After school ★ ★	After school ★ ★	After lunch	After lunch
Tell parent when OCD happens (reward for each instance)	After dinner	After dinner	After dinner ★	After dinner ★ ★	After dinner ★	After dinner	After dinner ★
Misc notes/bonus rewards					Ate muffin without complaint or checking; gave extra TV time		

Figure 5.6

Example of Completed Reward Chart

Therapist Note

▓ Depending on the child and family, it may make sense for this portion of the session to be presented to parents alone. ▓

Continue to discuss the concept of using positive attention (e.g., hugs, praise, and other rewards) to increase the desirable things that the child does. This could involve praising the child's successful attempts to take control of OCD, including monitoring symptoms, reporting symptoms to parents, and completing homework assignments. Eventually this positive attention will include praise for the child's attempts to "boss back" OCD. Additionally, parents should be praising or paying attention to the things that the child does or enjoys doing that are not related to OCD. Remind parents that we do not want the child to feel that the only attention he receives is because of his OCD. Next session will address removing attention—that is, trying to give less positive or negative attention to OCD-related struggles. You may use the following dialogue in your discussion:

> *As we talked about last week, differential attention is a powerful parenting tool that you are already using with your child every day. Last week we focused on the reward program, but today we want to talk about using other kinds of positive attention to increase the desirable things your child does. One of the ways that we pay attention to the good things kids do is by praising them. In what situations do you think you give your child a lot of praise?*
>
> *Giving positive attention to certain things that your child does may make those things more likely to occur in the future. Have you seen this happen with your child?*

Praise and OCD

Explain that praise is something that probably happens less often in relation to OCD because the symptoms are often confusing and frustrating. Rather than praise, parents give the child's OCD different kinds of attention. Parents often respond by trying to reassure and redirect the child, or they may try to set limits with the child to try to stop the struggle. When the symptoms are less severe (or absent), parents are often happy to "let sleeping dogs lie" and not refer to it for fear that saying something could make things worse. But OCD is a constant struggle and when symptoms are less severe are times when the child is more successful at managing his obsessions or compulsions. Encourage parents to think about paying attention to and praising their child for courageous behavior in which he is fighting back against OCD (e.g., praise going to a friend's house rather than praise lack of time spent washing hands). Sometimes, children with OCD feel as if they cannot do anything "good," so it is important for them to get positive attention for doing well in certain situations.

For this week, ask parents to give positive attention (specifically praise, encouragement, and hugs) when their child completes the assigned homework tasks. Over time they will be working on paying attention to their child's brave, nonanxious behavior they want to see more of.

Optional Role-Play

Have parents role-play the use of effective praise and encouragement. Parents should take turns playing the role of the parent and the child. You can also model these skills in role-plays first, if parents need more structure.

Level of Family Involvement

Last session, you and the parents discussed the ways in which family members are involved in specific OCD behaviors. Ask the parents the following questions:

- *Were you able to track this on your homework?*
- *Do you have any questions about this?*
- *Have you thought any more about how OCD impacts the family?*
- *Have you noticed anything different this week?*

Tell parents that they should keep approaching OCD-related requests as they usually do in the coming week. Provide rationale for keeping their level of involvement the same for the time being—with the exception of criticism, which should have been assessed and begun to be addressed as part of the process issue for Sessions 2. You may want to use the following dialogue:

> *Over the course of our treatment, we will be reducing some of this involvement very gradually using specific skills that you will learn during these sessions. That is why it is so important to keep careful track of your involvement at this stage of treatment.*
>
> *For right now, I pretty much just want you to continue to do what you normally would do in response to your child's behavior. This is very important because if you started changing your behavior all of the sudden, it could be very stressful for (child's name). By starting treatment, your child is making a big step toward fighting back against OCD, but it needs to be done in a gradual way.*

Homework

Monitoring:

✎ Have parents and child work together to monitor some aspect of the child's OCD symptoms. They may use the Monitoring Form or Reward Chart provided in the workbook.

Note: Younger children may not be able to participate in monitoring in a meaningful way. In these cases, parents can tell the child when they are marking a symptom on the chart in order to increase awareness of OCD.

For Parents:

✎ Have parents use praise, encouragement, sticker chart, and specific rewards for homework completion.

✎ Have parents track their responses to their child's OCD symptoms using the Session 3 homework sheet provided in the workbook.

For Child:

✎ Have child draw a picture of OCD and come up with a name for OCD, if appropriate, on the My OCD page in Chapter 3 of the workbook.

✎ Have child color or modify the feelings thermometer, if appropriate, on the My Feelings Thermometer page in Chapter 3 of the workbook.

Note: These tasks are not required to be assigned as homework. For children who are able to play a role in the self-monitoring, that can be their primary homework assignment. For younger children who are not doing self-monitoring, the drawing of OCD is a good assignment. The drawing can also be completed in the session.

Creating a New Hierarchy (Therapist Only)

Between this session and the next session, you should consolidate the information learned from the parents in Session 2 and from the parents and child in Session 3 onto a new hierarchy form. A blank Hierarchy Form 3 is provided in this chapter; you may photocopy as needed. See Figure 5.7 for an example of a form filled out before Session 4. The new form will organize the information learned to date into symptom complexes such that connections between specific triggers, obsessions, and compulsions are more explicit. Leave the ratings column blank so that this information can be obtained based on a new way of defining it to be presented in the next session.

Trigger	Obsession	Compulsion	Rating
Smelling cleaner, seeing the bottle, or seeing shiny or wet surfaces in the kitchen	Worries about being poisoned by household cleaners	Avoiding eating off recently cleaned surfaces	
Smelling cleaner, seeing the bottle, or seeing shiny or wet surfaces in the kitchen	Worries about being poisoned by household cleaners	Repeated questioning parents about use of cleaners (verbal checking)	
	Worries about mold on food	Examination of food for mold (self)	
	Worries about mold on food	Asking family member to examine food for mold	
	Worries about mold on food	Avoiding eating food that is likely to be moldy (e.g., bread, muffins)	
	Worries about whether he had swallowed objects (e.g., paper clip)		
	Worries about touching dirt on the floor		

Figure 5.7

Example of Pre-Session 4 Hierarchy Form 3

Hierarchy Form 3

Trigger	Obsession	Compulsion	Rating

Chapter 6   *Session 4: Family-Based Treatment*

(Corresponds to chapters 2, 3, and 4 of the workbook)

Materials Needed

- Hierarchy Form 3
- Feelings Thermometer
- Daily Practice Record

Outline

- Review past week
- Problem solve related to homework or reward program
- Continue to develop hierarchy of symptoms
- Introduce "bossing back" (child tool)
- Conduct in-session exposure
- Discuss differential attention, specifically ignoring (parent tool)
- Review level of family involvement in OCD symptoms
- Problem solve obstacles to homework compliance
- Assign homework

Review of Past Week

Answer any questions that have arisen in the previous week. Reward child's efforts and progress. Ask the following questions:

- *Do you have any questions from our last session?*

- *How was this past week? Were there any significant events?*

Problem Solving About Homework

Review symptom monitoring worksheets and complete immediate problem solving. Questions to ask may include the following:

- *Generally speaking, were there any problems?*

- *How did things go with the sticker chart?*

- *What might have worked better?*

- *What might you want to change for next week?*

- *Did you (child) bring in a picture of OCD and/or come up with a name for OCD?*

Continued Hierarchy Development

The purpose of this section is to review the hierarchy developed in the last session and make any necessary modifications. As you will have consolidated information obtained from parents and child over the preceding weeks into a new form (Hierarchy Form 3 at the end of Session 3), it is important to confirm that the way the information is now represented makes sense to the child and the parents. In particular, review carefully any places where you have made links among specifics triggers, obsessions, and compulsions that the child or family may not have explicitly stated in previous sessions. Use this reorganization of information to guide where further probing for symptom content is required (e.g., where there are obsessions without previously identified compulsions). This discussion will be significantly different depending on the child's developmental level (i.e., ability to understand the concept of ranking symptoms, ability to talk about the symptoms) and the nature of the child's symptoms.

Revising Ratings

In reviewing the hierarchy in preparation for doing E/RP tasks, it is important to carefully verify the feelings thermometer ratings that the child has given, making sure that the ratings correspond to the level of difficulty or fear the child anticipates when trying to alter or eliminate the ritual. This task has the potential to be confusing because previous feelings thermometer ratings may not have been obtained based on the same parameters. In other words, it is possible that the level of general distress or fear associated with a certain symptom is not the same as the distress or fear associated with trying to resist that ritual. For example, a child may rate the distress or fear associated with doing her handwashing ritual as a "4" but may rate the distress or fear associated with NOT doing (or resisting) this ritual as an "8." Specifically, examine ratings for all the items on the hierarchy that include rituals. For items where avoidance is the "ritual," ask how hard it would be not to avoid. You may want to use the following dialogue:

> *The feelings thermometer is one of our tools to fight against OCD—like we talked about last week, it lets us gain some control over OCD by helping to figure out which OCD symptoms bother us a lot and which OCD symptoms bother us less. Let's take a look at our list from last week. When we gave ratings last week, we were mostly focusing on how upset each symptom made you. As we look at it again this week, I want us to focus on what the ratings would be if we asked you to change or get rid of certain behaviors. Looking at ratings this way, does anyone think we need to make any changes?*

The following questions may also be helpful in rating hierarchy items based on trying to overcome the ritual:

- *If you didn't do (specific ritual) from hierarchy, how would you feel? What would your rating be?*

- *If you had to approach instead of avoid (specific avoided stimulus from hierarchy), how would you feel? What would your rating be?*

Add these ratings to the Hierarchy Form 3 completed between sessions or complete a new form if needed. See Figure 6.1 for an example of a completed form. An additional blank form is provided in this chapter.

Trigger	Obsession	Compulsion	Rating
Smelling cleaner, seeing the bottle, or seeing shiny or wet surfaces in the kitchen	Worries about being poisoned by household cleaners	Avoiding eating off recently cleaned surfaces	10
Smelling cleaner, seeing the bottle, or seeing shiny or wet surfaces in the kitchen	Worries about being poisoned by household cleaners	Repeated questioning parents about use of cleaners (verbal checking)	9
	Worries about mold on food	Examination of food for mold (self)	8
	Worries about mold on food	Asks family member to examine food for mold	8
	Worries about mold on food	Avoiding eating foods that are likely to be moldy (e.g., bread and muffins)	8
	Worries about whether she had swallowed objects (e.g., paper clip)	Repeatedly asking parents if he swallowed objects	8
	Worries about touching dirt on the floor	Avoiding certain objects on the floor	5

Figure 6.1

Example of Completed Hierarchy Form

Hierarchy Form 3

Trigger	Obsession	Compulsion	Rating

Obtaining Details

Hierarchy development also entails getting as many details about the child's OCD and associated triggers as possible. For example, specific objects, people, and places may be associated with especially high levels of anxiety and may be avoided to control that anxiety. Conversely, it is also important to learn about situations in which the child is less anxious or more willing to take risks. It is often helpful to ask very specific questions about the child's symptoms, modeling that it is safe to talk about the details here and demonstrating acceptance and understanding of the child. The process of fleshing out the details of the hierarchy should continue throughout treatment. The success of E/RP rests on the foundation of a detailed symptom hierarchy. It is not uncommon at this point in treatment to encounter a hierarchy that has ratings only at the high and low ends of the scale. The process of getting details about triggers and situations in which the child feels more and less anxious will help flesh out the middle ranges of the hierarchy.

Introduction to "Bossing Back"

The purpose of this section is to introduce cognitive strategies that will help with exposure, in particular, "bossing back" (March & Mulle, 1998) and positive self-talk. The key concepts to cover (particularly for younger children) are the following:

- What it means to be the boss or be in charge

- Therapist and parents are going to help the child be the boss of OCD

- Being the boss of OCD is hard work but we know the child can do it

Therapist Note

- *This section will need to be simplified depending on the cognitive and developmental level of the child. The following provides examples of therapist dialogue—although it might be too much information for children, it is often important for parents to hear to help them understand the concept of bossing back (so that they can help explain it to their child).* ▪

Present the information as in the following dialogue:

> *Today, we are going to talk about some other tools to fight OCD. We are going to learn about how to talk to OCD—"bossing back"—and we are going to learn some ways to talk to yourself to help you boss back OCD. Bossing back means talking back to OCD and telling it who is in charge. Sometimes this just means telling OCD that you know it is trying to control you (e.g., "I see what you're trying to do OCD, and I'm not going to fall for it."). Sometimes it means telling OCD that you don't believe what it is telling you. It can also mean telling OCD that you believe the opposite of what it is telling you. For example, if OCD told you that you would get sick if you touch the sink in the bathroom, you could tell OCD that you know you wouldn't get sick from touching the sink. Bossing OCD can be hard because OCD can be very sneaky. Sometimes when you start bossing it back, OCD might try new things to convince you that it's in charge. When this happens, it is a good idea to use more general ways of talking back to OCD. For example, instead of telling OCD that you won't get sick if you touch the sink you could tell OCD, "Back off, I'm the boss of me; you can't tell me what to do anymore."*
>
> *Another thing that will help you boss back OCD is keeping good thoughts about yourself in your head. When people think things like "I know I can't do this," or "What if I mess this up?" it is easier for OCD to keep bossing them around. But, when people think things like "I know it will be hard to face my fears, but I think I can; I will use my tools to help me; I can do this one step at a time," then they feel stronger and this helps them beat OCD. This kind of positive self-talk helps before, during, and after an exposure task.*

Bossing back OCD and using positive self-talk are important for parents to learn because it will help them support the child's efforts. It is also helpful because parents and other people in the child's life are often bossed around by OCD too.

In-Session Exposure

Conduct in-session practice exposure task (in vivo or imaginal; in vivo preferable) with parents present, if possible. You may introduce practice with the following dialogue:

> *Now that we have reviewed some things to help fight against (child's name for OCD), let's try using them here in the office! Let's pick something with a low temperature rating from our list and try to boss it back.*

Introduce the Daily Practice Record, which parents will use to record homework E/RP tasks. Have parents practice completing the form during in-session exposure. Forms are provided for parent use in the workbook. A copy is also provided in this chapter.

Choosing the Task

Choosing an appropriate task from the hierarchy is a crucial element of successful E/RP. Early in treatment, and in particular for the first experience with E/RP, the goal is to choose a task that will be well within the child's ability range. It is essential that the child feel successful and empowered by her experience during this task. The task chosen should produce a level of anxiety that is low enough that the child can tolerate it without much difficulty. The purpose of this E/RP task is to gather information and practice anxiety reduction before E/RP begins in earnest in the next session. The most reliable method to determine what is a tolerable level of anxiety for the child at this point in time is to explore the parts of the hierarchy where the child is sometimes successful in controlling the symptoms.

Preparing for the Task

Before doing the task, talk through the steps involved with the child and the family and give specific directions about resisting ritualizing. For example:

Daily Practice Record

Task Description:

Reminder of Specific Strategies to Use:

Thermometer Ratings

Date	What was attempted	Pre-task	1 min	2 min	5 min	10 min	15 min	20 min

Reward (describe what can be earned and what are the criteria for earning it):

We will go into the bathroom together, and when you touch the sink, I will ask you how high your feelings thermometer has gone up. Then, every 1–2 min I will ask you again how high your fear is until it has come all the way down to 1 or 0. The most important part is that you do not wash your hands or wipe them off in any way until your anxiety has come all the way down.

If parents appear upset at the prospect of E/RP, meet with them alone briefly to reinforce the importance of their encouragement and positive reaction. If the child resists doing exposure, you need to assess whether you have chosen something that is too difficult as an initial exposure. It is more important for the child to be "on-board" with the concept of doing exposures in session than for this task to be particularly anxiety provoking. Therefore, negotiate openly with the child to determine what task she would feel comfortable attempting today.

Completing the Task

Use feelings thermometer to make ratings every minute during the task. Continue exposure until the thermometer rating has gone down to 0 or 1 or the child is reporting a big decrease in anxiety. You may "coach" the child during the task by "talking back to OCD" for the child. Have parents observe and give the child positive reinforcement. With younger children, parents may need to assist more actively with the exposure task. Also, younger children will be less likely to give accurate ratings throughout the task; they may repeat themselves even if other indicators (e.g., facial expression and posture) suggest that their rating really should have changed. If possible, they can make ratings with pictures of faces or just tell you whether they are feeling better or worse.

If there is no practical item (due to nature of child's symptoms) that can be completed with an in-session E/RP task (either in vivo or imaginal), then time in session should be spent preparing in detail for the task to be completed at home.

Differential Attention (3): Removal of Attention

Work with the family to identify places where they may be able to begin to remove attention and disengage from child's symptoms (this will be somewhat case specific). Depending on the family's situation and the age of child, the child may play a more or less active role in this discussion (and may not be present for the entirety of this topic). The following dialogue may be helpful:

> *For the last two sessions, we have focused on ways to reward your child in order to help encourage her to act in desired ways. We have talked about using praise, encouragement, and other kinds of rewards (like prizes and stickers). We are now going to talk about the flip side of this idea—not paying attention to (or not rewarding) behavior that you don't want your child to be doing. In this way, you will try to reduce the amount of attention these behaviors get and make them less likely to occur. Over time, we will work on reducing reassurances, questions, and confrontations when your child is engaging in OCD symptoms.*

Stress to parents that the number one rule of removing attention is to never ignore a child if she is a danger to herself or anyone else. When removing attention from a behavior, parents should pick a behavior that does not have the possibility of being dangerous.

Explain that removal of attention means that parents cannot speak to their child, touch their child, or make eye contact with her. Once parents remove attention from a behavior, they have to continue to ignore it until she stops doing it. It will not be helpful if parents remove attention at first, and then pay attention to it once it has been going on for a while.

Level of Family Involvement

For homework this week, parents will work on removing attention for any complaints or refusals to do homework (E/RP). As far as all other symptoms, parents should continue to do what they have been doing for the most part. Emphasize, however, that it is important not to be critical or angry about these behaviors. Parents should remind themselves that their child is not doing these behaviors on purpose or to upset them.

Review homework for the past week in which parents kept track of their involvement in their child's symptoms. Use this time to talk about the direction parents will move in during upcoming sessions (e.g., reducing involvement in OCD symptoms). Review rationale for not doing this yet (i.e., it needs to be gradual so as not to create too much stress for the child). Slowly, over the course of this treatment program, parents will learn to boss back their part in OCD and begin to cut down their involvement in their child's symptoms.

Problem Solving Obstacles to Homework

Before assigning today's homework, discuss the potential for homework noncompliance and brainstorm ideas for how to handle resistance. Use the following dialogue:

> *Homework is a critical component to this treatment. What you "put in" in terms of homework will likely determine what you will "get out" of treatment over time. Even the best intentions for accomplishing homework can sometimes be difficult to meet. Can you think of some obstacles that could arise in trying to practice the skills we will be discussing in sessions? Based on what we have discussed so far, what are some ways of managing these obstacles?*

Look for parents to raise issues such as time or scheduling problems, interference from siblings, resistance from the child, etc. Depending on the particular family situation, solutions may include sharing responsibility between parents, using a consistent time for CBT practice when distractions are at a minimum, ignoring off-task behavior, etc. What is most important is that parents will use the reward plan and positive attention to increase incentive for homework compliance and reinforce on-task behavior, but have some strategies in mind for managing situational resistance.

Homework

For Parents:

✎ Have parents use positive attention for homework completion and removal of attention for complaints or refusals to do homework.

✎ Have parents track their responses to their child's OCD symptoms using the Session 4 homework sheet provided in the workbook.

For Child:

✎ Have child complete trial E/RP task each day, with parental help as appropriate. Exposures can be recorded on the Daily Practice Record; copies are provided in the workbook.

Note: Ideally, this will be the task (or some version of it) that was used in today's session. At this point in treatment, the goal of this exercise is to build the child and the family's confidence about doing E/RP. Because the therapist is not there to assist, the same task which produces one rating in the office may produce a higher rating at home. Thus, err on the side of choosing a task that is too easy rather than one that is too hard.

Chapter 7   *Session 5: E/RP / Modeling*

(Corresponds to chapters 2, 3, 4, and 5 of the workbook)

Materials Needed

- Hierarchy Form
- Feelings Thermometer
- Daily Practice Record

Outline

- Address therapy process issues throughout the session
- Review past week
- Problem solve related to homework tasks
- Revise hierarchy of symptoms (can be done in context of E/RP practice)
- Review cognitive strategies (can be done in context of E/RP practice)
- Conduct in-session exposure
- Discuss modeling (parent tool)
- Assign homework

Therapy Process Issues: Family Response to OCD

Throughout the session, continue to address or challenge family members' feelings of blame, guilt, or anger about the child's illness and to restructure negative thoughts regarding the child's OCD. Discuss parents' feelings about accommodation—especially their feelings about withdrawing involvement from their child's symptoms. This topic was initially introduced in Session 2 and is meant to be a process-oriented rather than didactic portion of treatment.

Different families will be very different with regard to accommodation, reaction, and response to child's OCD. It may also be relevant to explore areas of secondary gain (for child and for family) that may act as a barrier to success in treatment. The goal is to help families become more aware of these issues and eventually bring them to attention in therapy.

You will likely need to use recent events that occurred in and out of sessions to lead this discussion. You may incorporate the following questions:

- *As we have talked about before, everyone in the family can have different responses to OCD, sometimes being supportive about the symptoms and sometimes not. How is this going for everyone at your house?*

- *What did you notice when you tracked your accommodation of (child's name)'s symptoms?*

- *How would it feel to be less involved in (child's name)'s symptoms?*

Review of Past Week

Answer any questions that have arisen in the previous week. Reward child's efforts and progress. Ask the following questions:

- *Do you have any questions from our last session?*

- *How was this past week? Were there any significant events?*

Problem Solving About Homework

Review homework and complete immediate problem solving. Evaluate the trial exposure for treatment issues such as motivation, accuracy of predicting anxiety levels, parental involvement, and impact of comorbidities. Because premature bailing out of exposures ends up reinforcing OCD, pay particular attention to whether the child was able to stick with the task until anxiety levels dropped. Probe for signs of ritualizing (overt or covert) that could have caused anxiety levels to drop without habituation having occurred. Questions to ask may include the following:

- *Generally speaking, were there any problems?*

- *Were you (parents) able to use positive attention and removal of attention?*

- *How did it go with the trial exposure task?*

- *What might have worked better? What might you want to change for next week?*

Revision of Hierarchy

Review and revise the hierarchy developed in the last session. Add new symptoms and details about old symptoms, then revise ratings. Think about how family disengagement can be incorporated into the hierarchy. The purpose is to identify ways in which parents could very gradually begin to reduce accommodation. Try to get ratings for symptoms based on whether or not parents are involved. If possible, choose a symptom for practice this week that involves decreasing parent accommodation— even if you have to contrive the task. You may ask the following questions:

- *In what situations do you think you would be able to disengage yourself?*

- *What might this be like (or what was this like) for everyone involved?*

- *Do you foresee (or were there) any difficulties?*

- *Is there anything that makes sense to work on this week?*

Therapist Note

- *At this point in treatment, revising the hierarchy will likely be accomplished in the context of the E/RP task and/or in designing the homework assignment for the week. This requires clinical judgment as to what is best for the child and family given developmental level, nature and breadth of symptoms, ability to attend to multiple tasks within the session, etc. It does NOT need to be discussed as a separate treatment component from this session forward. If warranted and clinically indicated, however, continue to revise the hierarchy in a structured manner.* ▪

Review of Cognitive Strategies

Review cognitive strategies to help with exposure, specifically use of positive self-statements and "bossing back" strategies. Determine which phrases work for the child.

Note: These strategies may not work for younger children, as children may not want to say them out loud. Make suggestions about modifications as necessary. The extent to which children versus parents will discuss the use of these strategies will depend on the age of the child. The following questions may be helpful:

▪ *How have the strategies we talked about last week—bossing back OCD and saying positive things to yourself—been working?*

▪ *Does anyone think we need to make any changes?*

Therapist Note

▪ *At this point in treatment, it is very appropriate for this discussion to be accomplished in the context of the E/RP task (below). For most patients, it will make more sense to discuss "bossing back" strategies while planning/implementing the E/RP task rather than as a separate topic.* ▪

In-Session Exposure

Conduct in-session exposure task (in vivo or imaginal; in vivo preferable) with parents observing. Parents may fill out the Daily Practice Record.

Choosing the Task

Choose a new item on the hierarchy that allows for in-session E/RP and has a rating that is slightly higher than the one done for homework or in session last week. The rate and pattern of progress through the hierarchy across sessions will vary on a case-by-case basis. It is important to take into account the child's and the family's motivation level and success with previous in-session and homework assignments. It is sometimes necessary to repeat tasks from previous weeks rather than move on to new items on the hierarchy. Repetition is advised if there is doubt about whether the child and the family have sufficiently mastered their responses to a particular symptom cluster.

It is often the case that the symptoms for which family members have the most motivation are those that are causing the most distress, but these are often also the more difficult items on the child's hierarchy. Therefore, you must help the child and the family choose tasks that are attainable for the current point in treatment, while tying these tasks into their long-term goal of accomplishing tasks further up on the hierarchy. It may be necessary to contrive a task to achieve one with an appropriate rating.

Preparing for the Task

Before doing the task, talk through the steps involved with the child and the family and give specific directions about resisting ritualizing and using cognitive strategies. It is frequently helpful to overtly model the exposure task, for example touching a "contaminated" object.

If parents appear upset at the prospect of E/RP, meet with them alone briefly to reinforce the importance of their encouragement and positive reaction. If the child resists doing exposure, try to increase the child's motivation by telling him about other children his age who have been successful with similar items. If this is not successful, modify the task to make it possible for the child to participate.

Completing the Task

Use the feelings thermometer to make ratings every minute during the task. Continue exposure task until thermometer rating has gone down to 0 or 1 or the child is reporting a big decrease in anxiety. You may "coach" the child during the task by "talking back to OCD" for the child. Have the parents observe and give positive reinforcement. With younger children, parents may need to assist more actively with the exposure task. It is important to model for parents a calm, supportive, and encouraging presence during child exposure tasks.

Modeling

Note: In most cases, this section should be completed with the parents alone. Goals or key concepts for this section include the following:

- Children can learn both positive and negative behaviors by observing others (especially parents)

- Parents can model anxious behaviors or coping behaviors in reference to OCD

Let parents know that all parents teach their children good and bad things through their own behaviors or actions in certain situations (particularly when it comes to coping with difficult situations). Ask the parents the following questions:

- *When you are at your best, what do your children learn from watching you?*

- *When you are at your worst in a difficult situation (particularly an anxiety provoking one), what do they learn?*

Explain that sometimes parents do things, even unknowingly, which can add to OCD behaviors or feelings. Emphasize that you know that parents are not trying to do anything to exacerbate their child's symptoms but that a child's thoughts and feelings can be greatly affected by the things parents do. You may want to use the following dialogues to illustrate:

Parents can model all different kinds of behaviors for their children. There are probably many times when you are able to positively influence your child's behavior by modeling courageous or coping actions. For example, if your child is afraid of doing something (e.g., petting a large dog), you do it first, showing him that it is safe and

*saying positive things such as "I know this dog looks big, but we know
he is friendly because he is our neighbor's dog and I have petted him
before." This may help your child to feel better about the situation.*

*On the flip side, parents' own anxieties can affect their child. For
example, a child who is concerned about germs is about to enter a
public restroom. A parent may then heighten the child's anxiety by
warning the child to be careful while using the restroom. The child
may also pick up on behaviors of the parent regarding the cleanliness of
the restroom. If the parent says something like "Even though this might
not be the cleanest bathroom ever, we can use it anyway" in response to
the child's worries or uses the bathroom himself without displaying
concern, the parent is modeling that we go forward even if we are
anxious.*

Ask the parents whether they can think of any situations when they
might be stressed/tense/anxious and their behavior might influence their
child's symptoms. Explain that the goal of this treatment is that parents
will help their children by modeling ways to "talk back" or "boss back"
OCD. This will be talked about a lot in the weeks to come.

Optional Role-Play

Have parents role-play both helpful and unhelpful kinds of modeling
using situations that relate to their child. Parents should take turns playing the role of the parent and the child. You can also model these skills
in role-plays first, if parents need more structure.

Homework

For Parents:

✎ Have parents pay attention to their own modeling in relation to their
child's OCD.

✎ Have parents practice modeling coping skills in relation to a specific
OCD symptom if possible (e.g., parents model touching toilet in
public bathroom if this is a hard thing for the parents). *Note:* Pick a

symptom that makes sense for the parents, regardless of whether that situation is anxiety provoking for the child. Situations that are difficult or anxiety provoking for parents may not be related to the child's OCD symptoms, and may not be OCD-related at all.

✎ Have parents use praise, encouragement, rewards, and/or sticker chart for homework completion, and removal of attention for complaints or refusals to do homework.

✎ Have parents complete the Session 5 homework sheet provided in the workbook.

For Child:

✎ Have child complete E/RP task each day, with parental help as appropriate (might involve decreased parent accommodation). Exposures can be recorded on the Daily Practice Record; copies are provided in the workbook.

Note: For the reasons noted previously, pick a task that is on the easy side, perhaps one with which the child has already had some success. Exposure duration is not important at this point, except that the child must complete the task, that is, he must stick with it until his anxiety attenuates (i.e., until his temperature is down to a 0 or 1 if possible, and at least until the rating goes down by three-fourths as compared to where it started.) Remind the child to make thermometer ratings and use cognitive strategies.

Chapter 8 · *Session 6: E/RP / Introduction to Scaffolding*

(Corresponds to chapters, 2, 3, 4, and 5 of the workbook)

Materials Needed

- Hierarchy Form
- Feelings Thermometer
- Daily Practice Record

Outline

- Address therapy process issues throughout the session
- Review past week
- Problem solve related to homework tasks
- Review disengagement efforts
- Revise hierarchy (can be done in context of E/RP practice)
- Review cognitive strategies (can be done in context of E/RP practice)
- Introduce scaffolding (parent tool)
- Conduct in-session exposure
- Review specifics of scaffolding steps
- Discuss comorbidity and other therapy needs (optional)
- Assign homework

The goal is to decrease child's and parents' distress related to child's anxiety symptoms. Throughout the session, continue to address or challenge family members' feelings of blame, guilt, or anger about the child's illness and to restructure negative thoughts regarding the child's OCD. This topic was initially introduced in Session 2, re-introduced in the last session, and is meant to be a process-oriented rather than didactic portion of treatment.

Different families will be very different with regard to accommodation, reaction, and response to a child's OCD. It may also be relevant to explore areas of secondary gain (for child and for family) that may act as a barrier to success in treatment. The goal is to help families become more aware of these issues and eventually bring them to attention in therapy.

You will likely need to use recent events that occurred in and out of sessions to lead this discussion. Remind parents that everyone in the family can have different responses to OCD, sometimes being supportive about the symptoms and sometimes not, and ask how this has been going in the past week. If you need to be more directive, the following questions may be helpful:

- *Have you been able to change the ways in which you react to (child's name)'s OCD symptoms and other behaviors?*

- *Are there situations in which you still find yourself becoming distressed?*

- *What do you think you could do to change this?*

Help the parents with problem solving as needed throughout the session. A section focused on disengagement efforts is also included in this session.

Review of Past Week

Answer any questions that have arisen in the previous week. Reward child's efforts and progress. Ask the following questions:

- *Do you have any questions from our last session?*

- *How was this past week? Were there any significant events?*

Problem Solving About Homework

Review homework or E/RP task and complete immediate problem solving. Evaluate the exposure task for treatment issues such as motivation, accuracy of predicting anxiety levels, parental involvement, and impact of comorbidities. Because premature bailing out of exposures ends up reinforcing OCD, pay particular attention to whether the child was able to stick with the task until anxiety levels dropped. Probe for signs of ritualizing (overt or covert) that could have caused anxiety levels to drop without habituation having occurred. Questions to ask may include the following.

For Child:

- *How do you think things have been going with bossing back (child's name for OCD)?*

- *What things have been the hardest to work on so far?*

- *Are you feeling any better at home, at school, and with friends? (You may need to be more concrete for younger children)*

- *Generally speaking, were there any problems?*

- *How did it go with the symptom monitoring?*

For Parents:

- *Were you able to use modeling?*

- *How did it go with the exposure task?*

- *What might have worked better? What might you want to change for next week?*

Disengagement

Review disengagement efforts over the course of the last week and negotiate changes for the upcoming week. The child will play some role (if desired and appropriate) in this discussion. The following questions may be helpful:

> *How did things work over the last week in terms of staying out of (child's name)'s OCD symptoms?*

> *In what situations were you able to disengage yourself?*

> *What was this like for everyone involved? Were there any difficulties?*

Discuss further reducing parental involvement in or accommodation of symptoms where possible over the next week. Disengagement efforts will continue to be gradual. It will again tie into whatever symptoms are chosen to focus on with the homework.

Revision of Hierarchy

Review and revise the hierarchy developed in the last session. Add new symptoms and details about old symptoms, then revise ratings.

Therapist Note

> *As in Session 5, revising the hierarchy will likely be accomplished in the context of the E/RP task and/or in designing the homework assignment for the week.*

Review of Cognitive Strategies

Review use of positive self-statements and "bossing back" strategies. Determine which phrases work for the child. Make suggestions about modifications as necessary. The extent to which children versus parents will discuss the use of these strategies will depend on the age of the child. The following questions may be helpful:

> *How have these strategies—bossing back OCD and saying positive things to yourself—been working?*

> *Does anyone think we need to make any changes?*

Therapist Note

▪ *As in Session 5, for most patients, it will make more sense to discuss "bossing back" strategies while planning or implementing the E/RP task rather than as a separate topic.* ▪

Introduction to Scaffolding or Coaching

Scaffolding is a technique that parents can use to help an anxious child take more responsibility for her symptom management and, consequently, decrease parental involvement in that process. Expectations for the process of symptom management should correspond to the child's developmental capabilities. Older children are likely to be better able to respond to the use of scaffolding or coaching techniques in ways that generalize across situations. Older children may also be better able to express their thoughts or cognitions at each step in the process. Younger children may benefit from simple reminders about why the process is important and from a supportive, confident attitude from the parent.

Explain that part of having parents become less involved in their child's symptoms means giving children some more responsibility for certain behaviors (where appropriate). If parents often do a ritual for the child, one way of doing this is allowing the child to complete a ritual but making her do it herself. You may want to use the following dialogue:

> *By encouraging your child to take some responsibility for these behaviors, you are actually demonstrating that you have the confidence she will be able to "boss back" the OCD. This is a good time in treatment to think again about how you as parents can show support and encouragement (assuring that the child does not feel abandoned) while expecting more from your child at the same time.*

Explain that scaffolding is particularly helpful for situations in which parents' instinct would be to "rescue" their child because she is feeling anxious (e.g., giving the child permission to avoid doing an E/RP task or allowing the child to avoid a particular situation). The following dialogue may be helpful:

> *The scaffolding tool is something that helps parents to assist their kids in fighting back against OCD. The basic idea is that scaffolding is a way for you and your child to approach OCD behaviors and E/RP assignments. You have already started practicing this technique by helping your child with the E/RP task both in session and at home. Scaffolding is really a concrete set of steps for you to follow to help make a challenging E/RP task more doable for your child.*

After this general introduction, demonstrate scaffolding through in-session exposure before discussing each step of scaffolding in detail.

In-Session Exposure Task

Complete in-session exposure task (in vivo or imaginal; in vivo preferable), modeling scaffolding strategy for parents, if possible. You may introduce today's practice with the following dialogue:

> *We are going to practice a new task in the office again this week, but today we are going to highlight how to use the scaffolding steps. We will go through the steps in more detail after we do this task.*

The goal is to model scaffolding steps in an experiential manner: listening to child concerns, reviewing rationale for E/RP, choosing the task, reviewing tools, practicing the task, reviewing the results, and rewarding effort (you may need to model more or less depending on the specific child and family). Use the following directions as a guide for what needs to be accomplished. Parents may fill out the Daily Practice Record.

Choosing the Task

Choose a new item on the hierarchy that allows for in-session E/RP and has a rating that is slightly higher than the one done for homework or in session last week. For the purposes of modeling the scaffolding steps for parents, highlight the ways in which you are eliciting child feedback about her feelings and thoughts about doing the proposed task (Step 1: Find out how the child feels).

Again, the rate and pattern of progress through the hierarchy across sessions will vary on a case-by-case basis. Take into account motivation level and success with previous tasks to guide exposure choice. It may be necessary to contrive a task to achieve one with an appropriate rating.

Preparing for the Task

Before doing the task, talk through the steps involved with the child and the family and give specific directions about resisting ritualizing and using cognitive strategies. It is frequently helpful to overtly model the exposure task, for example touching a "contaminated" object.

For the purposes of modeling the scaffolding steps for the parents, highlight the ways in which this discussion promotes doing the exposure. Emphasize the concrete steps for approaching the situation. (Step 2: Brainstorm with the child how to approach rather than avoid the situation.)

If parents appear upset at the prospect of E/RP, meet with them alone briefly to reinforce the importance of their encouragement and positive reaction. If the child resists doing exposure try to increase the child's motivation by telling her about other children her age who have been successful with similar items. If this is not successful, modify the task to make it possible for the child to participate.

Completing the Task

Use the feelings thermometer to make ratings every minute during the task. Continue exposure until thermometer rating has gone down to 0 or 1 or child is reporting a big decrease in anxiety. You may "coach" the child during the task by "talking back to OCD" for the child. Have parents observe and give positive reinforcement. With younger children, parents may need to assist more actively with the exposure task. It is important to model for parents a calm, supportive, and encouraging presence during child exposure tasks. Note for parents that doing the exposure task accomplishes the third step of scaffolding (Step 3: Choose one of the options from Step 2 and act on it).

Model the final step of scaffolding (Step 4: Evaluate and reward) for parents by postprocessing how the E/RP task went. Provide praise (and possibly a tangible reward if one has been agreed upon prior to the task) for effort and note concrete things that could be done differently next time.

Scaffolding Steps

Next, go through the steps involved in using scaffolding. Because this technique is to be used in conjunction with E/RP practice for homework, make the steps specific to the E/RP homework assignment for this week. Next week, you can talk more about using this strategy in other situations. Decide what level of detail is appropriate for parents on a case-by-case basis. Some parents will be overwhelmed by reviewing the "steps"—simplify as appropriate. Emphasize that the goal is for parents to empathetically encourage approach rather than avoidance in the child. Present each step with the following statements in italics.

Step 1: Find out how the child feels (e.g., afraid, angry, or sad) and empathize with the child.

- *Help your child to identify her feelings and thoughts.*

- *Listen to what your child is saying and let her know that she has been heard.*

- *Help your child use the feelings thermometer to identify the level of distress that she is experiencing.*

Step 2: Brainstorm with the child how to approach rather than avoid the situation.

- *As a parent, you will be in charge of activating the child to do the E/RP task. Generate ideas about how to approach the situation.*

- *Talk with your child about her concerns and provide a rationale for doing E/RP ("Avoiding the OCD doesn't make it go away").*

- *Offer some reasons why doing E/RP would be a good thing versus a bad thing ("You'll be in charge, not the OCD," "the OCD wants you to believe that you can't do it") or, if possible, prompt the child to generate some of these ideas.*

- *Help reinforce the importance of E/RP—it is necessary to feel some anxiety in order to practice being the boss of OCD.*

Note: *It is important to meet kids where they are in this process (cognitively, emotionally). Praise your child for generating ideas and/or for listening to you. Decide on which tools you and your child can use to accomplish the task.*

Step 3: Choose one of the options from Step 2 and act on it.

- *Pick from the ideas generated on how to approach rather than avoid the situation.*

- *Follow through on the exposure task.*

Step 4: Evaluate and reward.

- *Review how the plan worked (or didn't work).*

- *Try to learn from mistakes.*

- *Reward your child for trying, no matter how it turned out.*

Note: *In addition to the anxious feelings that can be evoked by the E/RP task, young children can be very sensitive about their performance when trying new things. Therefore, parents should anticipate resistance to practicing and/or frustration when the practice does not go quite as planned. Try to remind your child that this is a skill that she is learning, similar to riding a bicycle, and that it will take some time to get "good" at it. What's most important is to try to practice regularly, to be honest about how it went, and to reward the child for making an effort to practice regardless of the outcome.*

Comorbidity and Other Therapy Needs (Optional)

If necessary, discuss additional therapy needs and issues related to comorbidity. You may use the following dialogue:

We are now at the half-way point with our treatment program and before we finish up today, I just wanted to check in about any issues that may not be getting enough attention in this treatment program. Do you have any concerns about symptoms that we are not addressing at this point?

This may also be a good time to address individual or couples' therapy needs of parents that have not yet been addressed.

Homework

For Parents:

✎ Have parents use differential reinforcement and modeling.

✎ Have parents use scaffolding strategy for child E/RP tasks as appropriate.

✎ Have parents continue disengagement as appropriate.

✎ Have parents use praise, encouragement, rewards, and/or sticker chart for homework completion, and removal of attention for complaints or refusals to do homework.

✎ Have parents complete the Session 6 homework sheet provided in the workbook.

For Child:

✎ Have child complete E/RP task each day, with parents using scaffolding techniques as appropriate. Remind child to make thermometer ratings and use cognitive strategies. Exposures can be recorded on the Daily Practice Record; copies are provided in the workbook.

Chapter 9   *Session 7: E/RP Using Parental Scaffolding*

(Corresponds to chapters 2, 3, 4, and 5 of the workbook)

Materials Needed

- Hierarchy Form
- Feelings Thermometer
- Daily Practice Record

Outline

- Address therapy process issues throughout the session
- Review past week
- Problem solve related to homework tasks
- Review disengagement efforts
- Revise hierarchy (can be done in context of E/RP practice)
- Review cognitive strategies (can be done in context of E/RP practice)
- Conduct in-session exposure
- Expand scaffolding strategy beyond E/RP practice
- Assign homework

Therapy Process Issues: Family Response to OCD

This session's process issues are identical to Session 6. Continue to use recent events in and out of session to lead discussion of parental responses to anxiety and restructuring of negative thoughts regarding the child's OCD.

Remind parents that everyone in the family can have different responses to OCD, sometimes being supportive about the symptoms and sometimes not, and ask how this has been going in the past week. If you need to be more directive, the following questions may be helpful:

- *Have you been able to change the ways in which you react to (child's name)'s OCD symptoms and other behaviors?*

- *Are there situations in which you still find yourself becoming distressed?*

- *What do you think you could do to change this?*

Help parents with problem solving as needed. You will talk further about their disengagement efforts later in the session.

Review of Past Week

Answer any questions that have arisen in the past week. Reward child's efforts and progress. Ask the following questions;

- *Do you have any questions from our last session?*

- *How was this past week? Were there any significant events?*

Problem Solving About Homework

Complete immediate problem solving related to homework and exposure tasks. Evaluate the exposure task for treatment issues such as motivation, accuracy of predicting anxiety levels, parental involvement, and impact of comorbidities. Because premature bailing out of exposures ends up reinforcing OCD, pay particular attention to whether the child was able to stick with the task until anxiety levels dropped. Probe for signs of ritualizing (overt or covert) that could have caused anxiety levels to drop without habituation having occurred. Questions to ask may include the following:

- *How did things go with the E/RP task and parent scaffolding?*

- *What about with the other parenting tools?*

- *Were there any problems? What might have worked better?*

- *What might you want to change for next week?*

Disengagement

Review disengagement efforts over the course of the last week and negotiate changes for the upcoming week. The child will play some role (if desired and appropriate) in this discussion. The following questions may be helpful:

- *How did things work over the last week in terms of staying out of (child's name)'s OCD symptoms?*

- *In what situations were you able to disengage yourself?*

- *What was this like for everyone involved? Were there any difficulties?*

Discuss further reducing parental involvement in or accommodation of symptoms where possible over the next week. Disengagement efforts will continue to be gradual. It will again tie into whatever symptoms are chosen to focus on with the homework.

Revision of Hierarchy

Review and revise the hierarchy developed in the last session. Add new symptoms and details about old symptoms, then revise ratings.

Therapist Note

As in recent sessions, revising the hierarchy will likely be accomplished in the context of the E/RP task and/or in designing the homework assignment for the week.

Review of Cognitive Strategies

Review cognitive strategies to help with exposure, specifically use of positive self-statements and "bossing back" strategies. Determine which phrases work for the child. Make suggestions about modifications as necessary. The extent to which children versus parents will discuss the use of these strategies will depend on the age of the child. The following questions may be helpful:

- *How have these strategies—bossing back OCD and saying positive things to yourself—been working?*

- *Does anyone think we need to make any changes?*

Therapist Note

At this point in treatment, for most patients, it will make more sense to discuss "bossing back" strategies while planning or implementing the E/RP task rather than as a separate topic.

In-Session Exposure Task

Conduct in-session exposure task (in vivo or imaginal; in vivo preferable) with parents observing and using scaffolding strategy, if possible. You may introduce today's practice with the following dialogue:

We are going to practice a new task in the office again this week, but we want you (parents) to take the lead with the scaffolding steps learned last session.

Help parents to move through the scaffolding steps (you may need to model more or less depending on specific child and family). Use the following directions as a guide for what needs to be accomplished. Parents may fill out the Daily Practice Record.

Choosing a Task

Choose a new item on the hierarchy that allows for in-session E/RP and has a rating that is slightly higher than the one done for homework or in session last week. Encourage the parents to use scaffolding Step 1 by eliciting child feedback about his feelings and thoughts about doing the proposed task. As in previous sessions, the rate and pattern of progress through the hierarchy across sessions will vary on a case-by-case basis. Take into account motivation level and success with previous tasks to guide choice. It may be necessary to contrive a task to achieve one with an appropriate rating.

Preparing for the Task

Before doing the task, talk through the steps involved with the child and the family and give specific directions about resisting ritualizing and using cognitive strategies. It is frequently helpful to overtly model the exposure task, for example touching a "contaminated" object. Encourage the parents to use scaffolding Step 2 by helping them make statements to the child that promote doing the exposure and helping them brainstorm with their child about how the situation will be approached.

If parents appear upset at the prospect of E/RP, meet with them alone briefly to reinforce the importance of their encouragement and positive reaction. If the child resists doing exposure, try to increase the child's motivation by telling him about other children his age who have been successful with similar items. If this is not successful, modify the task to make it possible for the child to participate.

Completing the Task

Use feelings thermometer to make ratings every minute during the task. Continue exposure until thermometer rating has gone down to 0 or 1 or child is reporting a big decrease in anxiety. You may "coach" the child during the task by "talking back to OCD" for the child. Help parents use the scaffolding steps during the task. With younger children, parents may need to assist more actively with exposure task. It is important to model for parents a calm, supportive, and encouraging presence during child exposure tasks.

Help parents use scaffolding Step 4 by facilitating, as necessary, a postprocessing discussion of how the E/RP task went. Encourage parents to provide praise (and possibly a tangible reward if one has been agreed upon prior to the task) for effort and help them problem solve with child about things that could be done differently next time.

Scaffolding or Coaching (2)

Tell parents that you are now going to go through the steps involved in using scaffolding again, but this time expand this tool to situations other than practicing a specific E/RP task. For example, when child gets anxious about an OCD-related concern when out of the house or not doing a planned E/RP task (e.g., using a public bathroom). Use an example specific to the child and family. Remind parents that the goal is to empathetically encourage approach rather than avoidance in the child.

Therapist Note

▧ *Earlier in the session you already engaged in discussion about how use of this tool worked for parents and child over the last week. Use the following information as needed. Again, make sure that you tailor these steps to work for the family. It may be necessary to simplify the steps or focus more on how to use them in an experiential manner during the E/RP task.* ▧

Present each step again, highlighting how to apply it to non-planned situations using the dialogues in italics.

Step 1: Find out how the child feels (e.g., afraid, angry, or sad) and empathize with the child.

The difference in this step from last week is that you must work with the child to identify the level of difficulty in the situation (last week dealt with a pre-picked E/RP task so the difficulty had already been established). It is important to have a conversation with your child and determine whether or not this situation is a task they will be able to approach, and this will depend on where your child is at with his treatment.

Step 2: Brainstorm with the child how to approach rather than avoid the situation.

Talk with your child about his concerns and help provide a rationale for doing E/RP ("Avoiding the OCD doesn't make it go away"). Offer some reasons why doing E/RP would be a good thing versus a bad thing ("You'll be in charge, not the OCD," "the OCD wants you to believe that you can't do it") or, if possible, prompt the child to generate some of these ideas. Help reinforce the importance of E/RP— it is necessary to feel some anxiety in order to be the boss of OCD. Note: it is important to meet kids where they are in this process (cognitively, emotionally). Praise your child for generating ideas and/or for listening to you. Decide on which tools you and your child can use to accomplish the task.

Again, the difference from last week is that we are practicing now for situations in which you had not planned a specific E/RP task. After deciding whether this is a task your child will be able to approach, you still may need to come up with modifications so that it is appropriate with regard to level of difficulty (e.g., touching something else that touched the public toilet). You and your child will need to balance a number of issues (e.g., being in a hurry or being in public where others may be around) while attempting to boss back OCD. It may be important for you and your child to develop a signal or sign to use with each other that means "this is a time to try and boss back OCD" so that this doesn't always need to be said out loud (e.g., in front of friends).

Step 3: Choose one of the options from Step 2 and act on it.

Pick an option, now go and do it! Follow through on the exposure task. Because you may be doing this in a situation that is not conducive to taking frequent ratings, be flexible in how closely you adhere to the process of doing the exposure. However, as with planned exposures, it is important to avoid premature bailing out. Therefore, if at all possible, stick with the situation until your child's anxiety has gone down significantly.

Step 4: Evaluate and reward.

Evaluate how the plan worked (or didn't work), and reward your child for trying. Remember, the experience of doing E/RP "on the fly" (i.e., when the child is not expecting it) may be difficult for some children. Sometimes, these difficulties will look like anxiety, and other times may present more like oppositional behavior. Therefore, listen carefully for your child's feelings associated with being taken off guard by being asked to do E/RP "out of the blue." Empathize with these feelings, noting how what your child has just tried is different from what he's done in session and for homework so far. Emphasize that doing E/RP "in real life" is very important for being in charge of OCD. Reward your child for his efforts.

If the exposure task did not work because of the difference in being out in public versus at home, parents and child should work together to problem solve and brainstorm other approaches.

Homework

For Parents:

✎ Encourage parents to make use of all parent tools (attention, modeling, and scaffolding).

✎ Have parents apply scaffolding to an anxiety situation other than a planned E/RP practice (if possible).

✎ Have parents use praise, encouragement, scaffolding, rewards, and/or sticker chart to help with homework completion. Parents should use removal of attention for complaints or refusals to do homework.

✎ Have parents complete the Session 7 homework sheet provided in the workbook. This includes generating a list of tools that have been most helpful and ways in which the tools are specifically helpful for their family. The goal is to increase parents' comfort level with the tools and help them to make the tools "their own."

For Child:

✎ Have child complete an E/RP task each day with parental help or scaffolding as appropriate. Remind child to make thermometer ratings and use cognitive strategies. Exposures can be recorded on the Daily Practice Record; copies are provided in the workbook.

Chapter 10   *Session 8: E/RP: Mid Hierarchy / Portability of Tools*

(Corresponds to chapters 2, 3, 4, and 5 of the workbook)

Materials Needed

- Hierarchy Form
- Feelings Thermometer
- Daily Practice Record

Outline

- Continue to address therapy process issues identified in other sessions as necessary during this session
- Review past week
- Problem solve related to homework tasks
- Review disengagement efforts
- Revise hierarchy (can be done in context of E/RP practice)
- Review cognitive strategies (can be done in context of E/RP practice)
- Conduct in-session exposure
- Address well-being of parents and other family members
- Review parenting tools
- Discuss the importance of being consistent in using tools
- Assign homework

Review of Past Week

Answer any questions that have arisen in the past week. Reward child's efforts and progress. Ask the following questions:

- *Do you have any questions from our last session?*
- *How was this past week? Were there any significant events?*

Problem Solving About Homework

Complete immediate problem solving related to homework or exposure tasks. Evaluate the exposure task for treatment issues such as motivation, accuracy of predicting anxiety levels, parental involvement, and impact of comorbidities. Because premature bailing out of exposures ends up reinforcing OCD, pay particular attention to whether the child was able to stick with the task until anxiety levels dropped. Probe for signs of ritualizing (overt or covert) that could have caused anxiety levels to drop without habituation having occurred. Questions to ask may include the following:

- *How did things go with the E/RP task and with parent scaffolding outside of a planned E/RP task?*
- *What about with the other parenting tools?*
- *Were there any problems? What might have worked better?*
- *What might you want to change for next week?*

Disengagement

Check-in with the parents about the family's disengagement from the child's symptoms. Emphasize the importance of continuing to reduce their involvement in or accommodation of the child's symptoms where possible (as part of E/RP task). You may ask the following questions:

- *How have things been working in terms of staying out of (child's name)'s OCD symptoms?*

In what situations were you able to disengage yourself?

What was this like for everyone involved? Were there any difficulties?

What are the remaining areas of family accommodation?

How do you think we can work on these areas this week (in conjunction with the E/RP task)?

Revision of Hierarchy

Review and revise the hierarchy developed in the last session. Add new symptoms and details about old symptoms, then revise ratings.

Therapist Note

As in recent sessions, revising the hierarchy will likely be accomplished in the context of the E/RP task and/or in designing the homework assignment for the week.

Review of Cognitive Strategies

Review cognitive strategies to help with exposure, specifically use of positive self-statements and "bossing back" strategies. Determine which phrases work for the child. Make suggestions about modifications as necessary. The extent to which children versus parents will discuss the use of these strategies will depend on the age of the child. The following questions may be helpful:

How have the strategies we talked about last week—bossing back OCD and saying positive things to yourself—been working?

Does anyone think we need to make any changes?

Therapist Note

At this point in treatment, for most patients, it will make more sense to discuss "bossing back" strategies while planning or implementing the E/RP task rather than as a separate topic.

Conduct in-session exposure task (in vivo or imaginal; in vivo preferable) with parents taking the lead and using scaffolding technique, if possible. Parents may fill out the Daily Practice Record.

Choosing the Task

Choose a new item on the hierarchy that allows for in-session E/RP and has a rating that is slightly higher than the one done for homework/in session last week. Encourage the parents to use scaffolding Step 1 by eliciting child feedback about her feelings and thoughts about doing the proposed task. It may be necessary to contrive a task to achieve one with an appropriate rating. Although progression through the hierarchy will vary on a case-by-case basis, the intention is to be selecting items from the moderate to high end of the hierarchy by this point in treatment. The decision about whether to move more rapidly versus more gradually toward the most difficult items on the hierarchy should be based on the child's and family's motivation and success with previous tasks at home and in session.

Preparing for the Task

Before doing the task, talk through the steps involved with the child and the family and give specific directions about resisting ritualizing and using cognitive strategies. It is frequently helpful to overtly model the exposure task, for example touching a "contaminated" object. Encourage the parents to use scaffolding Step 2 by helping them make statements to the child that promote doing the exposure and helping them brainstorm with their child about how the situation will be approached.

If parents appear upset at the prospect of E/RP, meet with them alone briefly to reinforce the importance of their encouragement and positive reaction. If the child resists doing exposure, try to increase the child's motivation by telling her about other children her age who have been successful with similar items. If this is not successful, modify the task to make it possible for the child to participate.

Completing the Task

Use the feelings thermometer to make ratings every minute during the task. Continue exposure until thermometer rating has gone down to 0 or 1 or child is reporting a big decrease in anxiety. You may "coach" the child during the task by "talking back to OCD" for the child. Help parents use the scaffolding steps during the task. With younger children, parents may need to assist more actively with the exposure task. It is important to model for parents a calm, supportive, and encouraging presence during child exposure tasks.

Help parents use scaffolding Step 4 by facilitating, as necessary, a post-processing discussion of how the E/RP task went. Encourage parents to provide praise (and possibly a tangible reward if one has been agreed upon prior to the task) for effort and help them problem solve with child about things that could be done differently next time.

Family Well-Being

Discuss the impact of a chronic problem on family well-being and the importance of addressing the well-being of individual family members. Focus on parents' awareness of their own needs in order to fully support their child. Emphasize that parents need to have time for themselves and support from others. In fact, this is a crucial part of family treatment. In addition, it is good for children to see parents taking care of themselves because it gives children permission to do the same. The following questions may be helpful:

- *Are you taking time for yourselves?*

- *Do you think that you are getting enough outside support?*

- *Are there any interests, hobbies, or pastimes that you have given up as a result of your child's OCD or other behavior problems?*

Review of Parenting Tools

Discuss the continued use of parenting tools. Review homework assignment given to parents about making the tools "their own." If possible, do this portion of session without the child's presence. Engage parents in a discussion of the E/RP task just completed in session. How does it feel for them to take the lead with the scaffolding? Ask the following questions:

- *How is it going using all the parenting tools at this point?*

- *Has it been possible to continue to use the tools simultaneously?*

- *Are there any specific problems?*

- *How does it feel to use the scaffolding tool in particular?*

Being Consistent

Discuss the importance of being consistent in coping with the child's OCD in all situations. Consistency is sometimes a problem when symptoms happen away from home.

Therapist Note

This may be more or less relevant for some families depending on how many E/RP tasks have involved public situations to date and depending on the specifics of the child's OCD.

The following questions may be helpful:

- *How has it been going coping consistently with OCD?*

- *Can you think of times when you were able to be consistent away from home?*

- *Can you think of times when there have been problems?*

- *Have the scaffolding steps been helpful?*

You may also want to use the following dialogue:

As we have mentioned before, one thing that is particularly important in bossing back OCD is that everyone is very consistent—otherwise OCD can be very tricky. So, this means that it is very important to behave in a similar way wherever you are. All of the parenting tools and child tools we have talked about should be pretty portable and good for use in other situations. Let's talk about what this might look like for your family. Are there places other than home where OCD sometimes acts up (e.g., relative's homes, stores, school, or place of worship)?

Help problem solve use of parent tools in the relevant situations.

Homework

For Parents:

✎ Have parents continue use of all parent tools. Parents should note how tools are working for child and for themselves (e.g., child's performance during E/RP and parents' coaching during E/RP).

✎ Have parents apply parent tools to OCD situation outside of home (if appropriate).

✎ Have parents use praise, encouragement, scaffolding, rewards, and sticker chart to help with homework completion. Parents should use removal of attention for complaints or refusals to do homework.

✎ Have parents complete the Session 8 homework sheet provided in the workbook.

For Child:

✎ Have child complete E/RP task each day with parental help or scaffolding as appropriate. Remind child to make note of thermometer ratings and use cognitive strategies. Exposures can be recorded on the Daily Practice Record; copies are provided in the workbook.

Chapter 11   *Session 9: E/RP: Mid Hierarchy / Extending Strategies*

(Corresponds to chapters 2, 3, 4, and 5 of the workbook)

Materials Needed

- ▨   Hierarchy Form
- ▨   Feelings Thermometer
- ▨   Daily Practice Record

Outline

- ▨   Address therapy process issues throughout the session
- ▨   Review past week
- ▨   Problem solve related to homework tasks
- ▨   Discuss extending parent tools to other settings and caregivers
- ▨   Review and discuss continued use of parent tools
- ▨   Revise hierarchy (can be done in context of E/RP practice)
- ▨   Review cognitive strategies (can be done in context of E/RP practice)
- ▨   Conduct in-session exposure
- ▨   Assign homework

Address the following issues as appropriate (as they come up in session). As it gets further in treatment from when these ideas were initially presented, it is good to re-initiate the discussion and ask the family whether they have any new questions. Discuss the family's understanding of these items one at a time.

- The definition of OCD and reasons for developing

- The difference between OCD and non-OCD symptoms

- The key areas of treatment

- The need for the child to have most of the responsibility for his OCD

- The need for the family to be supportive yet not engaged in symptoms

Generate process-oriented family discussion and make clarifications where necessary. Emphasize progress that child and family have made up until this point. Use positive problem-solving strategies to reduce criticism and hostility.

Also, review parents' abilities to problem solve when difficulties arise. The following questions may be helpful:

- *Do you think there are any areas where you (the parents) are still having difficulty coping with (child's name)'s symptoms?*

- *Are there particular situations that are more difficult (e.g., setting limits, helping child take responsibility, or dealing with issues of secondary gain)?*

- *How have you been managing your own reactions or distress related to the symptoms? Has this distress changed over time?*

- *Similarly, how have you been managing your own anxiety and/or distress and the way this may affect (child's name)'s thoughts about certain OCD symptoms?*

- *How do you feel about sharing your own and your child's experience with OCD with others?*

Review of Past Week

Answer any questions that have arisen in the past week. Reward child's efforts and progress. Ask the following questions:

- *Do you have any questions from our last session?*

- *How was this past week? Were there any significant events?*

Problem Solving About Homework

Complete immediate problem solving related to homework or exposure tasks. Evaluate the exposure task for treatment issues such as motivation, accuracy of predicting anxiety levels, parental involvement, and impact of comorbidities. Because premature bailing out of exposures ends up reinforcing OCD, pay particular attention to whether the child was able to stick with the task until anxiety levels dropped. Probe for signs of ritualizing (overt or covert) that could have caused anxiety levels to drop without habituation having occurred. Questions to ask include the following:

- *How did things go with the E/RP task and parent scaffolding?*

- *What about with the other parenting tools and using them in places other than at home?*

- *Were there any problems? What might have worked better?*

- *What might you want to change for next week?*

Extending Strategies

Review use of tools learned to date and discuss extending these strategies to other caretakers (e.g., relatives and teachers). The goal is to implement these strategies in other settings such as at school or at a relative's home. Explain that there needs to be consistency in handling OCD situations even when the child is in someone else's care. Although most children tend to give their parents a harder time than other caretakers, it is clearly important to develop strategies that others can use while caring for the child if problems arise with OCD.

Depending on the specifics of OCD outside the home, this section will be more or less appropriate for individual families. Even if previous assessment of this issue suggests that it is less relevant for a particular family, it is important to reassess the issue at this time. If less relevant for the family now, mention the importance of consistency across settings as an issue to keep in mind for the future.

This issue may touch on anxiety about disclosing information about the child's problem to people outside of the immediate family. Therefore, part of adequately covering this item may include discussion of feelings about disclosure.

The following questions may be helpful:

- *What situations might be most applicable to your family?*
- *How have you tried to manage these kinds of situations in the past?*
- *Has this changed since you began treatment?*
- *Do others have more difficulty coping with OCD symptoms or other behavioral problems?*
- *How do you feel about sharing this information with people outside of the immediate family?*
- *How could this disclosure be handled to make it most palatable and productive?*

Developing the specifics of this program will depend on the particular situation of the family. For example, it may include a daily report card for school or daycare (e.g., a sticker chart or notebook that would go back and forth between parents and teachers). It is important to help parents negotiate with their child's teacher if this is necessary. Another helpful strategy may be providing psychoeducation for caretakers. Parents may also want to develop reward plans that relatives can use with the child.

Review of Parenting Tools

Discuss parents' continued use of tools, ability to make the tools their own, and their thoughts about their role in the E/RP tasks. Review and emphasize the tools that seem most relevant to the family given the issues they have had in treatment. The following questions may be helpful:

- *Have you given any more thought to how to make the tools we have learned most helpful for your family?*

- *What have you noticed about how and when you are using the tools?*

Revision of Hierarchy

Review and revise the hierarchy developed in the last session. Add new symptoms and details about old symptoms, then revise ratings.

Therapist Note

- *As in recent sessions, revising the hierarchy will likely be accomplished in the context of the E/RP task and/or in designing the homework assignment for the week.*

Review of Cognitive Strategies

Review cognitive strategies to help with exposure, specifically use of positive self-statements and "bossing back" strategies. Determine which phrases work for the child. Make suggestions about modifications as necessary. The extent to which children versus parents will discuss the use of these strategies will depend on the age of the child. The following questions may be helpful:

- *How have these strategies—bossing back OCD and saying positive things to yourself—been working?*

- *Does anyone think we need to make any changes?*

Therapist Note

At this point in treatment, for most patients, it will make more sense to discuss "bossing back" strategies while planning or implementing the E/RP task rather than as a separate topic.

In-Session Exposure Task

Conduct in-session exposure task (in vivo or imaginal; in vivo preferable) with parents taking the lead and using scaffolding, if possible. Parents may fill out the Daily Practice Record.

Choosing the Task

Choose a new item on the hierarchy that allows for in-session E/RP and has a rating that is slightly higher than the one done for homework or in session last week. Encourage the parents to use scaffolding Step 1 by eliciting child feedback about his feelings and thoughts about doing the proposed task. Although progression through the hierarchy will vary on a case-by-case basis, the intention is to be selecting items from the moderate to high end of the hierarchy by this point in treatment. The decision about whether to move more rapidly versus more gradually toward the most difficult items on the hierarchy should be based on the child's and family's motivation and success with previous tasks at home and in session.

Preparing for the Task

Before doing the task, talk through the steps involved with the child and family, and give specific directions about resisting ritualizing and using cognitive strategies. It is frequently helpful to overtly model the exposure task, for example touching a "contaminated" object. Encourage the parents to use scaffolding Step 2 by helping them make statements to the child that promote doing the exposure and helping them brainstorm with their child about how the situation will be approached.

If parents appear upset at the prospect of E/RP, meet with them alone briefly to reinforce the importance of their encouragement and positive reaction. If the child resists doing exposure, try to increase the child's motivation by telling him about other children his age who have been successful with similar items. If this is not successful, modify the task to make it possible for the child to participate.

Completing the Task

Use the feelings thermometer to make ratings every minute during the task. Continue exposure until thermometer rating has gone down to 0 or 1 or child is reporting a big decrease in anxiety. You may "coach" the child during the task by "talking back to OCD" for the child. Help parents use the scaffolding steps during the task. With younger children, parents may need to assist more actively with the exposure task. It is important to model for parents a calm, supportive, and encouraging presence during child exposure tasks.

Help parents use scaffolding Step 4 by facilitating, as necessary, a post-processing discussion of how the E/RP task went. Encourage parents to provide praise (and possibly a tangible reward if one has been agreed upon prior to the task) for effort and help them problem solve with child about things that could be done differently next time.

Homework

For Parents:

✎ Have parents continue to use all parent tools, with monitoring of parent and child success with exposure homework.

✎ Have parents teach other caregivers how to manage OCD, if appropriate.

✎ Have parents use praise, encouragement, scaffolding, rewards, and sticker chart to help with homework completion. Parents should use removal of attention for complaints or refusals to do homework.

✎ Have parents complete the Session 9 homework sheet provided in the workbook.

For Child:

✎ Have child complete E/RP each day with parental help or scaffolding as appropriate. Remind child to make thermometer ratings and use cognitive strategies. Exposures can be recorded on the Daily Practice Record; copies are provided in the workbook.

Chapter 12   *Session 10: E/RP: Top of the Hierarchy /*
Preparation for Termination

(Corresponds to chapters 2, 3, 4, and 5 of the workbook)

Materials Needed

- ▦ Hierarchy Form
- ▦ Feelings Thermometer
- ▦ Daily Practice Record

Outline

- ▦ Address therapy process issues throughout the session
- ▦ Review past week
- ▦ Problem solve related to homework tasks
- ▦ Revise hierarchy (can be done in context of E/RP practice)
- ▦ Review cognitive strategies (can be done in context of E/RP practice)
- ▦ Conduct in-session exposure
- ▦ Review parent tools and discuss continued use
- ▦ Assign homework (and remind family that next session is in 2 weeks)

Therapy Process Issues: Family Problem Solving

Continue this session with a focus on family problem solving. Discuss specific family problems (related to child's OCD) that took place during the past week and how they handled them. Now that parent tools are in place, it is important to explore in more detail the ways in which parent distress or family conflict may continue to play a role in the child's OCD. You may begin with the following dialogue:

At this point in treatment, we have talked about a number of strategies to reduce family conflict (as well as criticism, anxiety, and hostility) around OCD symptoms at home. In fact, I feel confident that you have learned the strategies that you will need when such issues come up in the future.

Questions to ask the parents and child (if appropriate) include the following:

* *Can you think of anything that happened this past week involving family anger/hostility/conflict related to OCD symptoms (or other behaviors)?*

* *What about any situations in which parent anxiety or distress may have contributed to (child's name)'s mood or anxiety level?*

* *What about situations in which it was hard for (child's name) to boss back OCD?*

Push for parents to identify and solve these issues with minimal therapist assistance.

Review of Past Week

Answer any questions that have arisen in the past week. Reward child's efforts and progress. Ask the following questions:

* *Do you have any questions from our last session?*

* *How was this past week? Were there any significant events?*

Problem Solving About Homework

Complete immediate problem solving related to homework or exposure tasks. Evaluate the exposure task for treatment issues such as motivation, accuracy of predicting anxiety levels, parental involvement, and impact of comorbidities. Because premature bailing out of exposures ends up reinforcing OCD, pay particular attention to whether the child was able to stick with the task until anxiety levels dropped. Probe for signs of ritualizing (overt or covert) that could have caused anxiety levels to drop without habituation having occurred. Questions to ask may include the following:

- *How did things go with the E/RP task and parent scaffolding?*

- *What about with the other parenting tools and using them in places other than at home or with other caretakers?*

- *Were there any problems? What might have worked better?*

- *What might you want to change for next week?*

Revision of Hierarchy

Review and revise the hierarchy developed in the last session. Add new symptoms and details about old symptoms, then revise ratings.

Therapist Note

As in recent sessions, revising the hierarchy will likely be accomplished in the context of the E/RP task and/or in designing the homework assignment for the week.

Review of Cognitive Strategies

Review cognitive strategies to help with exposure, specifically use of positive self-statements and "bossing back" strategies. Determine which phrases work for the child. Make suggestions about modifications as necessary. The extent to which children versus parents will discuss the use of these strategies will depend on the age of the child. The following questions may be helpful:

- *How have these strategies—bossing back OCD and saying positive things to yourself—been working?*

- *Does anyone think we need to make any changes?*

Therapist Note

▪ *At this point in treatment, for most patients, it will make more sense to discuss "bossing back" strategies while planning or implementing the E/RP task rather than as a separate topic.* ▪

In-Session Exposure Task

Conduct in-session exposure task (in vivo or imaginal; in vivo preferable) with parents observing and using scaffolding, if possible. Again, have parents take the lead. Parents may also fill out the Daily Practice Record.

Choosing the Task

Choose a new item on the hierarchy that allows for in-session E/RP and has a rating that is slightly higher than the one done for homework or in session last week. Encourage the parents to use scaffolding Step 1 by eliciting child feedback about her feelings and thoughts about doing the proposed task. Although progression through the hierarchy will vary on a case-by-case basis, the intention is to be selecting items from the high end of the hierarchy by this point in treatment. Although there are two more sessions left before the end of treatment, it is ideal if the task chosen for this week could be at or very near the top of the hierarchy to allow sufficient time for mastery of this symptom before the end of treatment.

Preparing for the Task

Before doing the task, talk through the steps involved with the child and the family, and give specific directions about resisting ritualizing and using cognitive strategies. It is frequently helpful to overtly model the exposure task, for example touching a "contaminated" object. Encourage the parents to use scaffolding Step 2 by helping them make statements to their child that promote doing the exposure and helping them brainstorm with their child about how the situation will be approached.

If parents appear upset at the prospect of E/RP, meet with them alone briefly to reinforce the importance of their encouragement and positive reaction. If the child resists doing exposure, try to increase the child's motivation by telling her about other children her age who have been successful with similar items. If this is not successful, modify the task to make it possible for the child to participate.

Completing the Task

Use the feelings thermometer to make ratings every minute during the task. Continue exposure until thermometer rating has gone down to 0 or 1 or child is reporting a big decrease in anxiety. You may "coach" the child during the task by "talking back to OCD" for the child. Help parents use the scaffolding steps during the task. With younger children, parents may need to assist more actively with the exposure task. It is important to model for parents a calm, supportive, and encouraging presence during child exposure tasks.

Help parents use scaffolding Step 4 by facilitating, as necessary, a post-processing discussion of how the E/RP task went. Encourage parents to provide praise (and possibly a tangible reward if one has been agreed upon prior to the task) for effort and help them problem solve with child about things that could be done differently next time.

Review of Parent Tools

Discuss parents' continued use of tools, ability to make the tools their own, and their thoughts about their role in the E/RP tasks. Review and emphasize the tools that seem most relevant to the family given the issues they have had in treatment. The following questions may be helpful:

- *Have you given any more thought to how to make the tools we have learned most helpful for your family?*
- *What have you noticed about how and when you are using the tools?*

For Parents:

✐ Have parents continue to use all parent tools, with monitoring of parent and child success with exposure homework.

✐ Encourage parents to use praise, encouragement, scaffolding, rewards and/or sticker chart to help with homework completion. Parents should use removal of attention for complaints or refusals to do homework.

✐ Have parents complete the Session 10 homework sheet provided in the workbook.

For Child:

✐ Have child complete E/RP task each day with parental help or scaffolding as appropriate. Remind child to make note of thermometer ratings and use cognitive strategies. Exposures can be recorded on the Daily Practice Record; copies are provided in the workbook.

REMINDER: Schedule next session for 2 weeks from today.

Chapter 13 | *Session 11: E/RP: Top of the Hierarchy / Relapse Prevention*

(Corresponds to chapters 4, 5, and 6 of the workbook)

Materials Needed

- Hierarchy Form
- Feelings Thermometer
- Daily Practice Record

Outline

- Continue to address therapy process issues identified in other sessions as necessary during this session
- Review past 2 weeks
- Problem solve related to homework tasks
- Revise hierarchy (can be done in context of E/RP practice)
- Review cognitive strategies (can be done in context of E/RP practice)
- Conduct in-session exposure
- Discuss handling future problems with OCD and relapse prevention
- Plan for next session's graduation party
- Assign homework (and remind family that the final session is in 2 weeks)

Review of Past 2 Weeks

Answer any questions that have arisen in the past two weeks. Reward child's efforts and progress. Ask the following questions:

- *Do you have any questions from our last session?*

- *How were the past two weeks? Were there any significant events?*

Problem Solving About Homework

Complete immediate problem solving related to homework or exposure tasks. Evaluate the exposure task for treatment issues such as motivation, accuracy of predicting anxiety levels, parental involvement, and impact of comorbidities. Because premature bailing out of exposures ends up reinforcing OCD, pay particular attention to whether the child was able to stick with the task until anxiety levels dropped. Probe for signs of ritualizing (overt or covert) that could have caused anxiety levels to drop without habituation having occurred. Questions to ask include the following:

- *How did things go with the E/RP task and parent scaffolding?*

- *What about with the other parenting tools and using them in places other than at home or with other caretakers?*

- *Were there any problems? What might have worked better?*

- *What might you want to change for next week?*

Revision of Hierarchy

Review and revise the hierarchy developed in the last session. Add new symptoms and details about old symptoms, then revise ratings.

Therapist Note

- *As in recent sessions, revising the hierarchy will likely be accomplished in the context of the E/RP task and/or in designing the homework assignment for the week.*

Review of Cognitive Strategies

Review cognitive strategies to help with exposure, specifically use of positive self-statements and "bossing back" strategies. Determine which phrases work for the child. Make suggestions about modifications as necessary. The extent to which children versus parents will discuss the use of these strategies will depend on the age of the child.

The following questions may be helpful:

- *How have these strategies—bossing back OCD and saying positive things to yourself—been working?*

- *Does anyone think we need to make any changes?*

Therapist Note

- *At this point in treatment, for most patients, it will make more sense to discuss "bossing back" strategies while planning or implementing the E/RP task rather than as a separate topic.*

In-Session Exposure

Conduct in-session exposure task (in vivo or imaginal; in vivo preferable) with parents taking the lead and using scaffolding, if possible. Parents may also fill out the Daily Practice Record.

Choosing the Task

Choose a new item on hierarchy that allows for in-session E/RP. Although progression through the hierarchy will vary on a case-by-case basis, the intention is to be selecting items from the high end of the hierarchy by this point in treatment. Although there is one more session left before the end of treatment, it is ideal if the task chosen for this week could be at or very near the top of the hierarchy to allow sufficient time for mastery of this symptom before the end of treatment. Encourage the parents to use scaffolding Step 1 by eliciting child feedback about his feelings and thoughts about doing the proposed task.

Preparing for the Task

Before doing the task, talk through the steps involved with the child and the family, and give specific directions about resisting ritualizing and using cognitive strategies. It is frequently helpful for the therapist to overtly model the exposure task, for example touching a "contaminated" object. Encourage the parents to use scaffolding Step 2 by helping them make statements to their child that promote doing the exposure and helping them brainstorm with their child about how the situation will be approached.

If parents appear upset at the prospect of E/RP, meet with them alone briefly to reinforce the importance of their encouragement and positive reaction. If the child resists doing exposure, try to increase the child's motivation by telling her about other children her age who have been successful with similar items. If this is not successful, modify the task to make it possible for the child to participate.

Completing the Task

Use feelings thermometer to make ratings every minute during the task. Continue exposure task until thermometer rating has gone down to 0 or 1 or child is reporting big decrease in anxiety. You may "coach" the child during the task by "talking back to OCD" for the child. Help parents use the scaffolding steps during the task. With younger children, parents may need to assist more actively with the exposure task. It is important to model for parents a calm, supportive, and encouraging presence during child exposure tasks.

Help parents use scaffolding Step 4 by facilitating, as necessary, a post-processing discussion of how the E/RP task went. Encourage parents to provide praise (and possibly a tangible reward if one has been agreed upon prior to the task) for effort and help them problem solve with child about things that could be done differently next time.

The goal of this section is to help parents to think about other OCD-related issues that could arise in the future and how they could use the strategies discussed in therapy to address these problems. You may use the following dialogue:

> *One thing I want to emphasize in this session is how much you all have learned with regard to managing and coping with OCD over the course of treatment. This certainly does not mean you can avoid dealing with future problems, but instead that you have developed a number of skills to help you when issues arise.*

Review all of the major parenting tools and discuss how parents can use them to address future problems. The following questions may be helpful:

- *What do you think are the most effective strategies you have learned to date?*
- *Can you think of problems that might occur in the future?*
- *How do you think you would handle these problems?*

Help parents to go over a number of hypothetical situations and apply the strategies they have learned.

Relapse Prevention

Discuss with parents that OCD is a chronic disorder and that symptoms may return in stressful situations and that symptoms may return in a different form (e.g., washing instead of ordering ritual). You may use the following dialogue:

> *Even when we see significant improvement during the course of treatment, it is important to remember that OCD symptoms may return at some point. This is particularly true during stressful life events or other stressful periods of development. Given (child's name)'s young age, it is likely that some OCD symptoms may return. These may look identical to the symptoms we have seen at this point or may look somewhat different.*

Go over some important points to remember:

- Parents should watch more carefully for a return of OCD symptoms during stressful periods.

- Children should not be over-protected from stress.

- Family should use strategies learned in treatment to cope with symptoms (e.g., using tool kit and sticker chart) as well as more general stress management techniques (e.g., relaxation and deep breathing).

- It is very important to provide the child with significant support and encouragement during a period of symptom exacerbation and to remember that dealing with these symptoms early on may prevent them from becoming worse.

Dealing With Symptom Reappearance

The goal of this section is to educate parents about what they should do if symptoms reappear. Parents can do the following:

1. Try to figure out whether the child is aware of the symptoms.

2. Work with the child on exposure.

3. Provide support and encouragement to the child and use other parent tools.

4. Consider a booster treatment session or a follow-up phone call with the therapist to determine whether more intensive intervention is necessary.

Graduation Party Planning

Tell the family that the next session (in 2 weeks) will include a graduation party to celebrate the completion of treatment. Negotiate a plan with parents as to who will supply food and drinks. Inquire about whom it makes sense to invite or include (e.g., other family members in addition to parents). Questions to ask the child include the following:

- *What kinds of things would you like to eat or drink at the party?*

- *Who should be invited?*

- *Are there special games you would like to play?*

Homework

For Parents:

✎ Have parents continue to use all parent tools, with monitoring of parent and child success with exposure homework.

✎ Have parents use praise, encouragement, scaffolding, rewards, and/or sticker chart to help with homework completion. Parents should use removal of attention for complaints or refusals to do homework.

✎ Have parents complete the Session 11 homework sheet provided in the workbook.

For Child:

✎ Have child complete E/RP task each day with parental help or scaffolding as appropriate. Remind child to make note of thermometer ratings and use cognitive strategies. Exposures can be recorded on the Daily Practice Record; copies are provided in the workbook.

REMINDER: Schedule next session for 2 weeks from today.

Chapter 14 *Session 12: Review / Graduation Party*

(Corresponds to chapter 6 of the workbook)

Materials Needed

- Food and drinks for graduation party
- Certificate of Achievement or Diploma

Outline

- Review past week
- Problem solve related to homework tasks
- Review treatment and terminate
- Throw graduation party and present certificate of achievement

Review of Past Week

Answer any questions that have arisen in the past 2 weeks. Reward child's efforts and progress. Answer specific questions about relapse prevention. Ask the following questions:

- *Do you have any questions from our last session?*
- *How were the past 2 weeks? Were there any significant events?*
- *Do you have any specific questions about relapse prevention?*

Problem Solving About Homework

Complete immediate problem solving related to homework or exposure tasks. Evaluate the exposure task for treatment issues such as motivation, accuracy of predicting anxiety levels, parental involvement, and impact of comorbidities. Because premature bailing out of exposures ends up reinforcing OCD, pay particular attention to whether the child was able to stick with the task until anxiety levels dropped. Probe for signs of ritualizing (overt or covert) that could have caused anxiety levels to drop without habituation having occurred. Questions to ask include the following:

- *How did things go with the E/RP task and parent scaffolding?*

- *What about with the other parenting tools and using them in places other than at home or with other caretakers?*

- *Were there any problems? What might have worked better?*

- *Even with treatment ending, what might you continue to work on?*

Treatment Review and Termination

Course of Treatment

The goal of this section is to review the child's current level of symptomatology and course of treatment. If items remain on the hierarchy, discuss how family will continue with exposure on their own. Review with parents the procedure for conducting exposures, emphasizing the following points:

- Use the feelings thermometer to make ratings every minute during the task.

- Continue exposure task until thermometer rating has gone down to 0 or 1 or child is reporting a big decrease in anxiety.

- "Coach" the child during the task by "talking back to OCD" for the child.

- Be a calm, supportive, and encouraging presence during child exposure tasks.

Review of Tools

Briefly review the parent and the child tools used during treatment.

Child Tools

▪ Identifying and monitoring OCD symptoms

▪ Learning how to externalize ("boss back") OCD

▪ Using a feelings thermometer to rate anxiety

▪ Working with parents to develop a hierarchy and implement E/RP

Parent Tools

▪ *Differential attention*: using attention to change a child's behavior

    1. Tangible rewards (reward program)
    2. Praise and encouragement
    3. Removal of attention

▪ *Modeling*: becoming aware of how parent behavior influences child behavior

▪ *Scaffolding*: working alongside a child to change her emotional response to a certain event or situation and ultimately help her to respond in more adaptive and independent ways

You may do a quick run-through of the scaffolding steps:

Step 1: Find out how the child feels (e.g., afraid, angry, or sad) and empathize with the child.

Step 2: Brainstorm with the child how to approach rather than avoid the situation.

Step 3: Choose one of the options from Step 2 and act on it.

Step 4: Evaluate and reward.

Progress Review and Termination Issues

Remind the family about all of the progress that they have made during treatment. Note and reinforce specific positive changes made by both the child and the family in terms of symptoms, general functioning, and relationships. Have parents and child discuss what they have learned in treatment and how they feel about termination.

Ask both the parents and the child the following questions:

- *What do you think you have learned in treatment?*

- *How do you think you will be able to use what you have learned in the future?*

- *What will each family member do in the event that symptoms return?*

- *How do you feel about being done with treatment?*

Review how to recognize when symptoms return and what to do. Also schedule follow-up visits (we recommend a booster session at 3 months).

Graduation Party

Finish the session by having a party with the child and the family. Food and drinks (selected by child during Session 11) will be served. Present the child with a certificate of achievement (one is included in the workbook). The child can pick out a fun activity to complete with you and/or her family (e.g., playing a game or going for a walk).

Fidelity Checklists

Session 1: Introduction to the Treatment Program (Parents Only)

Fidelity Checklist

Child's Name: _____   Date: _____

Parents' Names: _____   _____

Directions: Rate your fidelity to each session element on a scale of 1 to 7, with 1 indicating poor fidelity and 7 indicating high fidelity.

___Address process issues throughout session

___Establish rapport with parents or caretakers

___Assess overall impact of OCD and related behaviors on family functioning

___Provide psychoeducation about OCD as a neurobehavioral disorder

___Discuss the family's knowledge of OCD and cognitive-behavioral treatment (CBT)

___Explain the development and course of OCD

___Explain obsessive-compulsive spectrum disorders and comorbidity

___Differentiate between OCD behaviors and non-OCD behaviors

___Give overview of the treatment program

___Assign homework

Notes:

Session 2: Laying the Groundwork (Parents Only)

Fidelity Checklist

Child's Name: _____   Date: _____

Parents' Names: _____   _____

Directions: Rate your fidelity to each session element on a scale of 1 to 7, with 1 indicating poor fidelity and 7 indicating high fidelity.

___Address process issues throughout session

___Review past week with parents

___Initiate development of OCD symptom hierarchy

___Give overview of child and parent tools for treatment

___Introduce differential attention

___Introduce reward plan

___Assign homework

Notes:

_____

_____

_____

_____

_____

_____

Session 3: Child Introduction to the Treatment Program

Fidelity Checklist

Child's Name: _____   Date: _____

Parents' Names: _____   _____

Directions: Rate your fidelity to each session element on a scale of 1 to 7, with 1 indicating poor fidelity and 7 indicating high fidelity.

___Establish rapport with child

___Review past week

___Introduce child to treatment program

___Introduce child to reward program

___Review OCD symptoms with child

___Introduce feelings thermometer and symptom tracking (child tools)

___Discuss differential attention, specifically praise and encouragement (parent tools)

___Review level of family involvement in OCD symptoms

___Assign homework

___Create a new hierarchy between sessions (therapist only)

Notes:

_____

_____

_____

_____

_____

_____

_____

Session 4: Family-Based Treatment

Fidelity Checklist

Child's Name: _____   Date: _____

Parents' Names: _____   _____

Directions: Rate your fidelity to each session element on a scale of 1 to 7, with 1 indicating poor fidelity and 7 indicating high fidelity.

___Review past week

___Problem solve related to homework or reward program

___Continue to develop hierarchy of symptoms

___Introduce "bossing back" (child tool)

___Conduct in-session exposure

___Discuss differential attention, specifically ignoring (parent tool)

___Review level of family involvement in OCD symptoms

___Problem solve obstacles to homework compliance

___Assign homework

Notes:

_____

_____

_____

_____

_____

_____

_____

Session 5: E/RP / Modeling

Fidelity Checklist

Child's Name: _____   Date: _____

Parents' Names: _____   _____

Directions: Rate your fidelity to each session element on a scale of 1 to 7, with 1 indicating poor fidelity and 7 indicating high fidelity.

___Address therapy process issues throughout session

___Review past week

___Problem solve related to homework tasks

___Revise hierarchy of symptoms (can be done in context of E/RP practice)

___Review cognitive strategies (can be done in context of E/RP practice)

___Conduct in-session exposure

___Discuss modeling (parent tool)

___Assign homework

Notes:

_____

_____

_____

_____

_____

_____

_____

Session 6: E/RP / Introduction to Scaffolding

Fidelity Checklist

Child's Name: _____   Date: _____

Parents' Names: _____   _____

Directions: Rate your fidelity to each session element on a scale of 1 to 7, with 1 indicating poor fidelity and 7 indicating high fidelity.

___Address therapy process issues throughout session

___Review past week

___Problem solve related to homework tasks

___Review disengagement efforts

___Revise hierarchy (can be done in context of E/RP practice)

___Review cognitive strategies (can be done in context of E/RP practice)

___Introduce scaffolding (parent tool)

___Conduct in-session exposure

___Review specifics of scaffolding steps

___Discuss comorbidity and other therapy needs (optional)

___Assign homework

Notes:

_____

_____

_____

_____

_____

_____

_____

Session 7: E/RP Using Parental Scaffolding

Fidelity Checklist

Child's Name: _____   Date: _____

Parents' Names: _____   _____

Directions: Rate your fidelity to each session element on a scale of 1 to 7, with 1 indicating poor fidelity and 7 indicating high fidelity.

___Address therapy process issues throughout session

___Review past week

___Problem solve related to homework tasks

___Review disengagement efforts

___Revise hierarchy (can be done in context of E/RP practice)

___Review cognitive strategies (can be done in context of E/RP practice)

___Conduct in-session exposure

___Expand scaffolding strategy beyond E/RP practice

___Assign homework

Notes:

_____

_____

_____

_____

_____

_____

_____

Session 8: E/RP: Mid Hierarchy / Portability of Tools

Fidelity Checklist

Child's Name: _____   Date: _____

Parents' Names: _____   _____

Directions: Rate your fidelity to each session element on a scale of 1 to 7, with 1 indicating poor fidelity and 7 indicating high fidelity.

___Continue to address therapy process issues identified in other sessions as necessary during this session

___Review past week

___Problem solve related to homework tasks

___Review disengagement efforts

___Revise hierarchy (can be done in context of E/RP practice)

___Review cognitive strategies (can be done in context of E/RP practice)

___Conduct in-session exposure

___Address well-being of parents and other family members

___Review parenting tools

___Discuss the importance of being consistent in using tools

___Assign homework

Notes:

_____

_____

_____

_____

_____

_____

_____

Session 9: E/RP: Mid Hierarchy / Extending Strategies

Fidelity Checklist

Child's Name: _____   Date: _____

Parents' Names: _____   _____

Directions: Rate your fidelity to each session element on a scale of 1 to 7, with 1 indicating poor fidelity and 7 indicating high fidelity.

___Address therapy process issues throughout session

___Review past week

___Problem solve related to homework tasks

___Discuss extending parent tools to other settings and caregivers

___Review and discuss continued use of parent tools

___Revise hierarchy (can be done in context of E/RP practice)

___Review cognitive strategies (can be done in context of E/RP practice)

___Conduct in-session exposure

___Assign homework

Notes:

_____

_____

_____

_____

_____

_____

_____

Session 10: E/RP: Top of the Hierarchy / Preparation for Termination

Fidelity Checklist

Child's Name: _____   Date: _____

Parents' Names: _____   _____

Directions: Rate your fidelity to each session element on a scale of 1 to 7, with 1 indicating poor fidelity and 7 indicating high fidelity.

___Address therapy process issues throughout session

___Review past week

___Problem solve related to homework tasks

___Revise hierarchy (can be done in context of E/RP practice)

___Review cognitive strategies (can be done in context of E/RP practice)

___Conduct in-session exposure

___Review parent tools and discuss continued use

___Assign homework (and remind family that next session is in 2 weeks)

Notes:

_____

_____

_____

_____

_____

_____

_____

Session 11: E/RP: Top of the Hierarchy / Relapse Prevention

Fidelity Checklist

Child's Name: _____   Date: _____

Parents' Names: _____   _____

Directions: Rate your fidelity to each session element on a scale of 1 to 7, with 1 indicating poor fidelity and 7 indicating high fidelity.

___Continue to address therapy process issues identified in other sessions as necessary during this session

___Review past 2 weeks

___Problem solve related to homework tasks

___Revise hierarchy (can be done in context of E/RP practice)

___Review cognitive strategies (can be done in context of E/RP practice)

___Conduct in-session exposure

___Discuss handling future problems with OCD and relapse prevention

___Plan for next session's graduation party

___Assign homework (and remind family that the final session is in 2 weeks)

Notes:

_____

_____

_____

_____

_____

_____

_____

Session 12: Review / Graduation Party

Fidelity Checklist

Child's Name: _____   Date: _____

Parents' Names: _____   _____

Directions: Rate your fidelity to each session element on a scale of 1 to 7, with 1 indicating poor fidelity and 7 indicating high fidelity.

___Review past week

___Problem solve related to homework tasks

___Review treatment and terminate

___Throw graduation party and present certificate of achievement

Notes:

_____

_____

_____

_____

_____

_____

_____

_____

_____

Family Accommodation and Impact Scale–Child (FAIS-C)

(Adapted from the Family Accommodation Scale (FAS); Calvocoressi, et al., 1999)

Patient information sheet for assisting in the implementation of the Family Accommodation and Impact Scale-Child (FAIS-C).

MAJOR OBSESSIONS

1. _____

2. _____

3. _____

4. _____

5. _____

6. _____

7. _____

8. _____

9. _____

10. _____

MAJOR COMPULSIONS

1. _____

2. _____

3. _____

4. _____

5. _____

6. _____

7. _____

8. _____

9. _____

10. _____

IMPACT OF (THE CHILD'S) OCD ON THE FAMILY

THERAPIST DIALOGUE:
You have told me (your child) has the following symptoms (review). Now I am going to ask you about the impact these symptoms have had on your family members and quality of life.

Item 1. IMPACT OF OCD ON THE FAMILY

(Your child's) OCD may lead to . . .	No impact on life	A little impact on life	Some impact on life	A lot of impact on life	Very, very much of an impact on life
a) avoidance of certain places.					
b) little desire to go out					
c) time lost from work because of a need to take care of (your child)					
d) your family growing apart					
e) fights with your spouse					
f) losing time that could be spent on other activities					
g) a lot of waiting for (your child) (e.g. late for school or other places)					
h) inconvenience around the house (e.g. the bathroom being used for a long period of time)					
i) neglecting other siblings					
j) more fighting between the children					
k) school grades of (your child) to suffer					
l) fatigue					
m) inability to plan for the future					
n) modifying personal routine					
o) conflict among family members due to differences in modification of personal routine					

Item 2. DISTRESS/CRITICISM ASSOCIATED WITH ACCOMMODATION

When you do the things for (your child) that you have described to me, do you become upset, angry, or critical of (your child)? To what extent?

(Focus specifically on distress experienced and anger/criticism expressed when engaged in behaviors designed to accommodate the child, as distinguished from distress associated with the more general problem of the child having OCD.)

*If yes, specify:*_____

_____

_____

_____

2a. (RATER SCORED) How distressed does the parent become when accommodating the child?

    0 = Not at all
    1 = Mild, slight emotional distress
    2 = Moderate, definite emotional distress, but manageable
    3 = Severe, prominent emotional distress
    4 = Extreme, incapacitating emotional distress

2b. (RATER SCORED) How critical of the child does the parent become when accommodating the child?

    0 = Not at all
    1 = Mild, slight anger/criticism expressed
    2 = Moderate, definite anger/criticism expressed
    3 = Severe, significant anger/criticism expressed
    4 = Extreme, extreme anger/criticism expressed

PARENT RESPONSES TO OBSESSIONS, COMPULSIONS, AND RELATED SYMPTOMS

You have told me that (your child) has the following symptoms (review). I am now going to ask you about the ways you may have responded to (your child) and his/her symptoms during the past week.

(When you feel it is needed it may aid the parent if you use the CY-BOCS to formulate concrete examples for specific items. (e.g.

Have you helped (your child) undertake or complete compulsions? For example, you noted that (your child) washes her hands many times per day. Do you buy extra soap for her?))

Item 3. PROVIDING REASSURANCE

Have you reassured (your child) when he/she expresses worries, fears, or doubts related to obsessions or compulsions?

(Reassurance that disturbing thoughts are unfounded or that the child cleaned or checked enough are included here.)

Is this reassurance part of your child's compulsions, such as in the form of verbal checking? Who initiates this reassurance? Does (your child) ask for the reassurance or do you provide it in anticipation of (your child's) obsessions and compulsions?

If yes, specify: _____

_____

_____

_____

3a. How many times did you reassure (your child) during the past week?

    0 = Never
    1 = Mild, 1/week
    2 = Moderate, 2–3/week
    3 = Severe, 4–6/week
    4 = Extreme, every day

Note specific number of times/week reported by family member:_____

3b. On average, how many reassurances did you give (your child) each time you reassured him/her this past week?

    0 = None
    1 = Mild, 1–2 reassurances/interaction
    2 = Moderate, 3–6 reassurances/interaction
    3 = Severe, 7–10 reassurances/interaction
    4 = Extreme, > 10 reassurances/interaction

Note specific number of reassurances reported by family member:_____

3c. On average, during the past week, how much time did you spend reassuring (your child)?

> 0 = Never
> 1 = Mild, less than 1 hr/week
> 2 = Moderate, 1–3 hr/week
> 3 = Severe, 3–5 hr/week
> 4 = Extreme, >5 hr/week

Note average time/week reported by family member:_____

Item 4. TOLERATING CHILD'S ABERRANT BEHAVIOR, INCLUDING HAVING TO REFRAIN FROM SAYING/DOING THINGS

During the past week, have you put up with things (your child) has done that you would prefer that he/she not do?

(OCD-related behaviors that are a hardship for the relative are included here; e.g., the child's excessive use of the bathroom, or having stacks of newspapers, or mail in the house that the child cannot discard.)

In addition, are there things that you do not do or say because of (your child's) OCD? (Specific behaviors such as refraining from physical contact with family members or not entering certain areas of the home would be included here.) *Who initiates this refrain? Does your child ask you not to or do you do so in anticipation of your child's response?*

*If yes, specify:*_____

_____

_____

_____

4a. (RATER SCORED) To what extent, during the past week, did the family member tolerate odd behaviors?

> 0 = Not at all
> 1 = Mild, tolerated slightly unusual behavior
> 2 = Moderate, tolerated behavior that is somewhat odd
> 3 = Severe, tolerated very unusual behavior
> 4 = Extreme, tolerated extremely aberrant behavior

Item 5. FACILITATING COMPULSIONS AND PARTICIPATING IN COMPULSIONS

During the past week, have you helped (your child) undertake or complete compulsions?

(Behaviors such as providing the child with clean towels, or buying excessive quantities of soap are included here.)

Additionally, have you engaged in compulsions or behaviors which you consider odd or senseless at (your child's) request? (Include washing/cleaning, checking, repeating, ordering; e.g., parent checks the stove if patient is afraid of fire.) *Who initiates these behaviors (such as did your child ask you to buy soap or did you buy it of your own accord)?*

*If yes, specify:*_____

_____

_____

_____

5a. How often, during the past week, did you help (your child) undertake/complete rituals?

0 = Never
1 = Mild, 1/week
2 = Moderate, 2–3/week
3 = Severe, 4–6/week
4 = Extreme, every day

Note specific number of times/week reported by family member:_____

5b. How much time, on average, did you spend each time you helped (your child) undertake/complete rituals?

0 = None
1 = Mild, < 10 min/episode
2 = Moderate, > 10 and < 20 min/episode
3 = Severe, > 20 and < 30 min/episode
4 = Extreme, > 30 min/episode

Note specific amount of time reported by family member in minutes:_____

5c. On average, during the past week, how much time did you spend helping (your child) undertake/complete rituals?

 0 = None
 1 = Mild, less than 1 hr/week
 2 = Moderate, 1–3 hr/week
 3 = Severe, 3–5 hr/week
 4 = Extreme, > 5 hr/week

Note average time/week reported by family member:_____

Item 6. FACILITATING AVOIDANCE

Do you assist (your child) in avoiding people, places, or things?

(Include only those behaviors that specifically relate to the child's avoidance, e.g., telling friends the patient is not home if patient is avoiding social contacts.)

For example, who initiated these behaviors? Did (your child) ask you to assist him/her or did you initiate assistance in anticipation of (your child's) actions?

*If yes, specify:*_____

_____

_____

_____

6a. How often, during the past week, did you help (your child) avoid things?

 0 = Never
 1 = Mild, 1/week
 2 = Moderate, 2–3/week
 3 = Severe, 4–6/week
 4 = Extreme, every day

Note specific number of times/week reported by family member:_____

6b. How much time, on average, did you spend each time you helped (your child) avoid things?

 0 = None
 1 = Mild, < 10 min/episode
 2 = Moderate, > 10 and < 20 min/episode

3 = Severe, > 20 and < 30 min/episode

4 = Extreme, > 30 min/episode

Note specific amount of time reported by family member in minutes:_____

6c. On average, during the past week, how much time did you spend helping (your child) avoid things?

0 = None

1 = Mild, less than 1 hr/week

2 = Moderate, 1–3 hr/week

3 = Severe, 3–5 hr/week

4 = Extreme, > 5 hr/week

Note average time/week reported by family member:_____

Item 7. HELPING THE CHILD WITH SIMPLE TASKS OR DECISIONS

Do you help (your child) complete simple tasks or make simple decisions when OC symptoms interfere with his/her ability to do so?

(Helping the child get dressed, or to decide what to eat are examples of behaviors included here.)

Do you initiate these behaviors in anticipation of (your child's) actions or does (your child) ask for this help?

*If yes, specify:*_____

_____

_____

_____

7a. How often during the past week, did you help (your child) with simple tasks/decisions?

0 = Never

1 = Mild, 1/week

2 = Moderate, 2–3/week

3 = Severe, 4–6/week

4 = Extreme, every day

Note specific number of times/week reported by family member:_____

7b. How much time, on average, did you spend each time you helped (your child) with simple tasks/decisions?

0 = None
1 = Mild, < 10 min/episode
2 = Moderate, > 10 and < 20 min/episode
3 = Severe, > 20 and < 30 min/episode
4 = Extreme, > 30 min/episode

Note specific amount of time reported by family member in minutes:_____

7c. On average, during the past week, how much time did you spend helping (your child) with simple tasks/decisions?

0 = None
1 = Mild, less than 1 hr/week
2 = Moderate, 1–3 hr/week
3 = Severe, 3–5 hr/week
4 = Extreme, >5 hr/week

Note average time/week reported by family member:_____

Item 8. TAKING ON THE CHILD'S RESPONSIBILITIES

Do you currently do some of the things for the family that would be (your child's) responsibility if he/she did not have OCD; for example, picking up his/her toys or cleaning his/her room? Who initiates this behavior? Does (your child) ask you to complete his/her responsibilities or do you do it of your own accord?

*If yes, specify:*_____

_____

_____

_____

8a. (RATER SCORED) To what extent has the family member taken on (your child's) responsibilities?

0 = Not at all
1 = Mild, occasionally handles one of patient's responsibilities, but no substantial change in role
2 = Moderate, has assumed patient's responsibilities in one area

3 = Severe, has assumed patient's responsibilities in more than one area

4 = Extreme, has assumed most or all of patient's responsibilities

PERCEPTIONS AND CONSEQUENCES OF FAMILY ACCOMMODATION

THERAPIST DIALOGUE FOR THE PARENT:

You have told me that you do the following things for (your child) (review above). I am now going to ask you about the effects that doing these things has on you and your child, and about what would happen if you discontinued your involvement.

Item 9 and 10. PERCEPTION OF EFFECT OF ACCOMMODATION

Item 9. Do you think that the things you do for (your child) help to improve his/her symptoms?

0 = Not at all

1 = May lead to a slight improvement in OCD symptoms

2 = Do help somewhat to improve OCD symptoms

3 = Definitely improve symptoms

4 = Essential to symptom improvement

Item 10. Do you think that the things you do for (your child) help him/her to function better?

0 = Not at all

1 = May lead to a slight improvement in functioning

2 = Do help patient to function somewhat better

3 = Definitely improve functioning

4 = Essential to improved functioning

Item 11, 12, and 13. CONSEQUENCES OF LIMITING ACCOMMODATION

Item 11. Would (your child) become anxious or distressed if you did not do these things.

0 = No

1 = Mild, child might complain of anxiety/distress, but his/her distress would not be too disturbing

2 = Moderate, child would experience definite distress, but he/she would be able to manage distress

3 = Severe, child would experience very definite distress and might pace or appear agitated

4 = Extreme, child would experience near constant or disabling distress

Has this actually happened? (circle one) yes no

Item 12. Would (your child) become angry or abusive if you did not do these things?

0 = No

1 = Mild, child would become slightly angry

2 = Moderate, child would become moderately angry and hostile

3 = Severe, child would become verbally abusive and threatening

4 = Extreme, child would become physically abusive

Has this actually happened? (circle one) yes no

Item 13. Would (your child) spend more time completing his/her rituals if you did not do these things?

0 = No

1 = Mild, an *increase* of less than 1 hr per day

2 = Moderate, an *increase* of more than 1 and less than 3 hr per day

3 = Severe, an *increase* of more than 3 and less than 8 hr per day

4 = Extreme, an *increase* of more than 8 hr per day

Has this actually happened? (circle one) yes no

Children's Yale-Brown OC Scale (CY-BOCS)
Self-Report Symptom Checklist

Children's Yale-Brown OC Scale (CY-BOCS) Self-Report Symptom Checklist

Name of Child: _____ Date: _____ Informant: _____

This questionnaire can be completed by the child/adolescent, parents, or both working together. We are interested in getting the most accurate information possible. There are no right or wrong answers. Please just answer the best you can. Thank you.

Please check all <u>COMPULSIVE</u> SYMPTOMS that you have noticed during the past week.

<u>COMPULSIONS</u> are things you feel compelled to do even though you may know the behavior does not make sense. Compulsions are typically done to reduce fear of distress associated with obsessive thoughts.

Washing/Cleaning Compulsions

_____ Excessive or ritualized hand washing (e.g., takes long time to wash, needs to restart if interrupted, needs to wash hands in particular order of steps)

_____ Excessive or ritualized showering, bathing, tooth brushing, grooming, toilet routine (see hand washing)

_____ Excessive cleaning of items (e.g., clothes, faucets, floors or important objects)

_____ Other measures to prevent or remove contact with contaminants (e.g., using towel or foot to flush toilet or open door; refusing to shake hands; asking family members to remove insecticides, garbage)

_____ Other washing/cleaning compulsions (Describe)_____

_____

Checking Compulsions

_____ Checking locks, toys, schoolbooks/items, and so on

_____ Checking associated with getting washed, dressed, or undressed

_____ Checking that did not/will not harm others (e.g., checking that nobody's been hurt, asking for reassurance, or telephoning to make sure that everything is alright)

_____ Checking that did not/will not harm self (e.g., looking for injuries or bleeding after handling sharp or breakable objects, asking for reassurance that everything is alright)

_____ Checking that nothing terrible did/will happen (e.g., searching the newspaper or television for news about catastrophes)

_____ Checking that did not make a mistake (e.g., while reading, writing, doing simple calculations, homework)

_____ Checking tied to health worries (e.g., seeking reassurance about having an illness, repeatedly measuring pulse, checking for body odors or ugly features)

_____ Other checking compulsions (Describe)_____

Repeating Compulsions

_____ Rereading, erasing, or rewriting (e.g., taking hours to read a few pages or write a few sentences because of concern over not understanding or needing letters to be perfect)

_____ Needing to repeat routine activities (e.g., getting up and down from a chair or going in and out of a doorway, turning the light switch or TV on and off a specific number of times)

_____ Other repeating compulsions (Describe)_____

Counting Compulsions

_____ Counts objects (e.g., floor tiles, CDs or books on a shelf, his/her own steps, or words read or spoken)

Arranging/Symmetry

_____ Arranging/ordering (e.g., spends hours straightening paper and pens on a desktop or books in a bookcase, becomes very upset if order is disturbed)

_____ Symmetry/evening up (e.g., arranges things or own self so that two or more sides are "even" or symmetrical)

_____ Other arranging compulsions (Describe)_____

Hoarding/Saving Compulsion (do not count saving sentimental or needed objects)

_____ Difficulty throwing things away; saving bits of paper, string, old newspapers, notes, cans, paper towels, wrappers and empty bottles; may pick up useless objects from street or garbage

_____ Other hoarding/saving compulsions (Describe)_____

Excessive Games/Superstitious Behaviors (must be associated with anxiety, not just a game)

_____ Behaviors such as not stepping on cracks or lines on floor/sidewalk, touching an object/self a certain number to times to avoid something bad happening, not leaving home on the 13th of the month)

Rituals Involving Other Persons

_____ Needing to involve another person (usually a parent) in rituals (e.g., excessive asking for reassurance, repeatedly asking parent to answer the same question, making parent wash excessively)

Miscellaneous Compulsions

_____ Excessive telling, asking, or confessing (e.g., confessing repeatedly for minor or imagined transgressions, asking for reassurance)

_____ Measures (not checking) to prevent harm to self or others or some other terrible consequences (e.g., avoids sharp or breakable objects, knives, or scissors)

_____ Ritualized eating behaviors (e.g., arranging food, knife, fork in a particular order before eating; eating according to a strict ritual)

_____ Excessive touching, tapping, rubbing (e.g., repeatedly touching particular surfaces, objects, or other people, perhaps to prevent a bad occurrence)

_____ Excessive list making

_____ Needing to do things (e.g., touch or arrange) until it feels "just right"

_____ Avoiding saying certain words (e.g., goodnight or goodbye, person's name, bad event)

_____ Other (Describe)_____

Please check all <u>OBSESSIVE</u> SYMPTOMS that you have noticed during the past week.

<u>OBSESSIONS</u> are intrusive, recurrent, and distressing thoughts, sensations, urges, or images that you may experience. They are typically frightening and may be either realistic or unrealistic in nature.

Contamination Obsessions

_____ Excessive concern with dirt, germs, certain illnesses (e.g., from door handles, other people)

_____ Excessive concern/disgust with bodily waste or secretions (e.g., urine, feces, semen, sweat)

_____ Excessive concern with environmental contaminants (e.g., asbestos or radioactive substances)

_____ Excessive concern with contamination from household items (e.g., cleaners, solvents)

_____ Excessive concern about contamination from touching animals/insects

_____ Excessively bothered by sticky substances or residues (e.g., adhesive tape, syrup)

_____ Concerned will get ill as a result of being contaminated by something (e.g., germs, animals, cleaners)

_____ Concerned will get others ill by spreading contaminant

_____ Other washing/cleaning obsessions (Describe)_____

_____

Aggressive Obsessions

_____ Fear might harm self (e.g., using knives or other sharp objects)

_____ Fear might harm others (e.g., fear of pushing someone in front of a train, hurting someone's feelings, causing harm by giving wrong advice)

_____ Fear something bad will happen to self

_____ Fear something bad will happen to others

_____ Violent or horrific images (e.g., images of murders, dismembered bodies, other disgusting images)

_____ Fear of blurting out obscenities or insults (e.g., in public situations like church, school)

_____ Fear will act on unwanted impulses (e.g., punch or stab a friend, drive a car into a tree)

_____ Fear will steal things against his or her will (e.g., accidentally "cheating" cashier or shoplifting something)

_____ Fear will be responsible for terrible event (e.g., fire or burglary because didn't check locks)

_____ Other aggressive obsessions (Describe)_____

Hoarding/Saving Obsessions

_____ Worries about throwing away unimportant things because he or she might need them in the future, urges to pick up and collect useless things

Health-Related Obsessions

_____ Excessive concern with illness or disease (e.g., worries that he or she might have an illness like cancer, heart disease, or AIDS despite reassurance from doctors; concerns about vomiting)

_____ Excessive concern with body part or aspect of appearance (e.g., worries that his or her face, ears, nose, arms, legs, or other body part is disgusting or ugly)

_____ Other health-related obsessions (Describe)_____

Religious/Moral Obsessions

_____ Overly concerned with offending God or other religious objects (e.g., having blasphemous thoughts, saying blasphemous things, or being punished for these things)

_____ Excessive concern with right/wrong, morality (e.g., worries about always doing "the right thing," worries about having told a lie or having cheated someone)

_____ Other religious obsessions (Describe)_____

Magical Obsessions

_____ Has lucky/unlucky numbers, colors, words, or gives special meaning to certain numbers, colors, or words (e.g., red is a bad color because once had a bad thought while wearing red shirt)

Sexual Obsessions

_____ Forbidden or upsetting sexual thoughts, images, or impulses (e.g., unwanted images of violent sexual behavior toward others, or unwanted sexual urges toward family members or friends)

_____ Obsessions about sexual orientation (e.g., that he or she may be gay or may become gay when there is no basis for these thoughts)

_____ Other sexual obsessions (Describe)_____

Miscellaneous Compulsions

_____ Fear of doing something embarrassing (e.g., appearing foolish, burping, having "bathroom accident")

_____ The need to know or remember things (e.g., insignificant things like license plate numbers, bumper stickers, T-shirt slogans)

_____ Fear of saying certain things (e.g., because of superstitious fears, fear of saying "thirteen")

_____ Fear of not saying the right thing (e.g., fear of having said something wrong or not using "perfect" word)

_____ Intrusive (nonviolent) images (e.g., random, unwanted images that come into his or her mind)

_____ Intrusive sounds, words, music, or numbers (e.g., hearing words, songs, or music in his or her mind that can't stop; bothered by low sounds like clock ticking or people talking)

_____ Uncomfortable sense of incompleteness or emptiness unless things done "just right"

_____ Other obsessions (Describe)_____

Adapted from Goodman, W. K., Price, L. H., Rasmussen, S. A., Riddle, M. A., & Rapoport, J. L. (1991). *Children's Yale-Brown Obsessive Compulsive Scale (CY-BOCS)*. New Haven, CT: Yale Child Study Center.

References

Abramowitz, J. S., Whiteside, S. P., & Deacon, B. J. (2005). The effectiveness of treatment for pediatric obsessive-compulsive disorder: A meta-analysis. *Behavior Therapy, 36*, 55–63.

American Psychological Association. (2000). *Diagnostic and statistical manual of mental disorders: DSM-IV-TR* (4th ed.), text revision. Washington, DC: Author.

Calvocoressi, L., Mazure, C., Kasl, S. V., Skolnick, J., Fisk, D., Vegso, S. J. et al. (1999). Family accommodation of obsessive-compulsive symptoms. *Journal of Nervous and Mental Disease, 187*(10), 636–642.

Evans, D. W., Leckman, J. F., Carter, A., Reznick, J. S., Henshaw, D., King, R. A. et al. (1997). Ritual, habit, and perfectionism: The prevalence and development of compulsive-like behavior in normal young children. *Child Development, 68*(1), 58–68.

Flament, M. F., Koby, E., Rapoport, J. L., Berg, C. J., Zahn, T., Cox, C. et al. (1990). Childhood obsessive-compulsive disorder: A prospective follow-up study. *Journal of Child Psychology and Psychiatry, 31*(3), 363–380.

Flament, M. F., Whitaker, A., Rapoport, J. L., Davies, M., Berg, C. Z., Kalikow, K., et al. (1988). Obsessive compulsive disorder in adolescence: An epidemiological study. *Journal of the American Academy of Child & Adolescent Psychiatry, 27*(6), 764–771.

Francis, G., & Gragg, R. A. (1996). Childhood obsessive compulsive disorder. In A. E. Kazdin (Ed.), *Developmental clinical psychology and psychiatry* (Vol. 35). Thousands Oaks: Sage Publications.

Garcia, A. M., Freeman, J. B., Himle, M. B., Berman, N. C., Ogata, A. K., Ng, J., et al. (in press). Phenomenology of early childhood onset obsessive compulsive disorder. *Journal of Psychopathology and Behavioral Assessment*.

Geller, D. A., Biederman, J., Griffin, S., Jones, J., & Lefkowitz, T. R. (1996). Comorbidity of juvenile obsessive-compulsive disorder with disruptive behavior disorders. *Journal of the American Academy of Child and Adolescent Psychiatry, 35*(12), 1637–1646.

Goodman, W. K., Price, L. H., Rasmussen, S. A., Mazure, C., Delgado, P., Heninger, G. R. et al. (1989). The yale-brown obsessive compulsive scale. II. Validity. *Archives of General Psychiatry*, *46*(11), 1012–1016.

Goodman, W. K., Price, L. H., Rasmussen, S. A., Mazure, C., Fleischmann, R. L., Hill, C. L. et al. (1989). The yale-brown obsessive compulsive scale. I. Development, use, and reliability. *Archives of General Psychiatry*, *46*(11), 1006–1011.

Goodman, W. K., Price, L. H., Rasmussen, S. A., Riddle, M. A., & Rapoport, J. L. (1991) *Children's Yale-Brown Obsessive Compulsive Scale (CY-BOCS)*. New Haven, CT: Yale Child Study Center.

Holzer, J. C., Goodman, W. K., McDougle, C. J., Baer, L., Boyarsky, B. K., Leckman, J. F. et al. (1994). Obsessive-compulsive disorder with and without a chronic tic disorder. *British Journal of Psychiatry*, *164*, 469–473.

Kaufman, J., Birmaher, B., Brent, D., Rao, U., Flynn, C., Moreci, P., et al. (1997). Schedule for Affective Disorders and Schizophrenia for School-Age Children-Present and Lifetime version (K-SADS-PL): Initial reliability and validity data. *Journal of the American Academy of Child & Adolescent Psychiatry*, *36(7)*, 980–988.

Kendall, P. C., Flannery-Schroeder, E., Panichelli-Mindel, S. M., Southam-Gerow, M., Henin, A., & Warman, M. (1997). Therapy for youths with anxiety disorders: A second randomized clinical trial. *Journal of Consulting and Clinical Psychology*, *65*(3), 366–380.

Kraemer, H. C., & Kupfer, D. J. (2006). Size of treatment effects and their importance to clinical research and practice. *Biological Psychiatry*, *59*, 990–996.

Last, C. G., Hansen, C., & Franco, N. (1998). Cognitive-behavioral treatment of school phobia. *Journal of the American Academy of Child and Adolescent Psychiatry*, *37*(4), 404–411.

Leckman, J. F., Goodman, W. K., North, W. G., Chappell, P. B., Price, L. H., Pauls, D. L. et al. (1994). The role of central oxytocin in obsessive compulsive disorder and related normal behavior. *Psychoneuroendocrinology*, *19*(8), 723–749.

Leckman, J. F., & Peterson, B. S. (1993). The pathogenesis of Tourette's syndrome: Epigenetic factors active in early CNS development. *Biological Psychiatry*, *34*, 425–427.

Leonard, H. L., Goldberger, E. L., Rapoport, J. L., Cheslow, D. L., & Swedo, S. E. (1990). Childhood rituals: Normal development or obsessive-compulsive symptoms? *Journal American Academy of Child & Adolescent Psychiatry*, *29*(1), 17–23.

Leonard, H. L., Lenane, M., & Swedo, S. E. (1993). Obsessive-compulsive disorder. *Child and Adolescent Psychiatric Clinics of North America, 2*(4), 655–665.

Leonard, H. L., Lenane, M. C., Swedo, S. E., Rettew, D. C., Gershon, E. S., & Rapoport, J. L. (1992). Tics and Tourette's disorder: A 2- to 7-year follow up of 54 obsessive-compulsive children. *American Journal of Psychiatry, 149*(9), 1244–1251.

March, J. S., & Leonard, H. L. (1998). Obsessive-compulsive disorder in children and adolescents. In R. P. Swinson, M. M. Antony, S. Rachman, & M. A. Richer (Eds.), *Obsessive-compulsive disorder: Theory, research, and treatment* (pp. 367–394). New York, NY: Guilford Press.

March, J., & Mulle, K. (1998). *OCD in children and adolescents: A cognitive-behavioral treatment manual.* New York: Guilford Press.

Pauls, D. L., Hurst, C. R., Kruger, S. D., Leckman, J. F., Kidd, K. K., & Cohen, D. J. (1986). Gilles de la Tourette's syndrome and attention deficit disorder with hyperactivity. *Archives General Psychiatry, 43,* 1177–1179.

Pediatric OCD Treatment Study Team [POTS]. (2004). Cognitive-behavior therapy, sertraline, and their combination with children and adolescents with obsessive-compulsive disorder: The Pediatric OCD Treatment Study (POTS) randomized controlled trial. *Journal of the American Medical Association, 292*(16), 1969–1976.

Piacentini, J., Bergman, R. L., Keller, M., & McCracken, J. (2003). Functional impairment in children and adolescents with obsessive-compulsive disorder. *Journal of Child and Adolescent Psychopharmacology, 13*(Suppl. 1), S61–S69.

Piacentini, J., Jacobs, C., & Maidment, K. (1998). *Individual CBT and family (ERP/Family) treatment: A multicomponent treatment program for children and adolescents with obsessive-compulsive disorder.* Unpublished manuscript.

Piacentini, J., Langley, A., & Roblek, T. (2007). *Cognitive-behavioral treatment of childhood OCD: Its only a false alarm, therapist guide.* New York: Oxford University Press.

Pina, A., Silverman, W., Weems, C., Kurtines, W., & Goldman, M. (2003). A comparison or completers and noncompleters of exposure-based cognitive and behavioral treatment for phobia and anxiety disorders in youth. *Journal of Consulting and Clinical Psychology, 71*(4), 701–705.

Pollack, R. A., & Carter, A. S. (1999). The familial and developmental context of obsessive-compulsive disorder. In R. A. K. L. Scahill (Ed.), *Obsessive compulsive disorder: Child and adolescent psychiatric clinics of North America* (Vol. 8, pp. 461–479). Philadelphia: W.B. Saunders.

Rapoport, J. L., Inoff-Germain, G., Weissman, M. M., Greenwald, S., Narrow, W. E., Jensen, P. S. et al. (2000). Childhood obsessive-compulsive disorder in the NIMH MECA Study: Parent versus child identification of cases. *Journal of Anxiety Disorders, 14*(6), 535–548.

Scahill, L., Riddle, M. A., McSwiggan-Hardin, M., Ort, S. I., King, R. A., Goodman, W. K. et al. (1997). Children's yale-brown obsessive-compulsive scale: Reliability and validity. *Journal of the American Academy of Child and Adolescent Psychiatry, 36,* 844–852.

Silverman, W. K., & Albano, A. M. (1996). *The Anxiety Disorders Interview Schedule for Children for DSM-IV: Child and Parent Versions.* San Antonio, TX: The Psychological Corporation.

Silverman, W. K., Kurtines, W. M., Ginsburg, G. S., Weems, C. F., Lumpkin, P. W., & Carmichael, D. H. (1999). Treating anxiety disorders in children with group cognitive-behaviorial therapy: A randomized clinical trial. *Journal of Consulting and Clinical Psychology, 67*(6), 995–1003.

Stark, L. J. (2003). *Be in charge: Behavioral intervention for change around growth and energy—Parent Manual.* Cincinnati, OH; Children's Hospital Medical Center, University of Cincinnati College of Medicine.

Stein, R. E. K., & Riessman, C. K. (1978). The Impact on Family Scale. (Available from Ruth E. K. Stein, M. D., Department of Pediatrics, Albert Einstein College of Medicine/Children's Hospital at Montefiore Medical Center, 111 East 210 Street, Bronx, NY, 10467).

Swedo, S. E., Rapoport, J. L., Leonard, H. L., Lenane, M., & Cheslow, D. (1989). Obsessive compulsive disorders in children and adolescents: Clinical phenomenology of 70 consecutive cases. *Archives of General Psychiatry, 46,* 335–343.

Valderhaug, R., & Ivarsson, T. (2005). Functional impairment in a clinical sample of Norwegian and Swedish children and adolescents with obsessive-compulsive disorder. *European Child and Adolescent Psychiatry, 14,* 164–173.

Valleni-Basile, L. A., Garrison, C. Z., Jackson, K. L., Waller, J. L. McKeown, R. E., Addy, C.L,, et al. (1994). Frequency of obsessive-compulsive disorder in a community sample of young adolescents. *Journal of the American Academy of Child & Adolescent Psychiatry, 33*(6), 782–791.

Woods, D. W., Piacentini, J., Chang, S., Deckersbach. T., Ginsburg, G., Peterson, A., et al. (2008). *Managing tourette's syndrome: A behavioral intervention for children and adults, therapist guide.* New York: Oxford University Press, Inc.

About the Authors

Jennifer B. Freeman, PhD, is Assistant Professor (Research) at the Warren Alpert Medical School of Brown University, Co-director of the Pediatric Anxiety Research Clinic (PARC) at the Bradley/Hasbro Children's Research Center, and Staff Psychologist at Rhode Island Hospital. She received her PhD in Clinical Psychology from the State University of New York at Buffalo and completed her internship and postdoctoral training through the Brown University Clinical Psychology Training Consortium. She and Henrietta Leonard, MD founded PARC in 2001. She is currently the Principal Investigator of two multisite treatment outcome studies for pediatric obsessive-compulsive disorder (OCD) from the National Institute of Mental Health. Dr. Freeman is an active CBT supervisor and teacher at Brown University for both psychology and psychiatry trainees. Her other research interests include the role that family dynamics play in childhood anxiety disorders. Dr. Freeman has presented and published articles on the treatment of OCD.

Abbe Marrs Garcia, PhD, is Assistant Professor (Research) at the Warren Alpert Medical School of Brown University, Co-director of the Pediatric Anxiety Research Clinic at the Bradley/Hasbro Children's Research Center, and Staff Psychologist at Rhode Island Hospital. She received her PhD in Clinical Psychology from Temple University and completed her internship and postdoctoral training through the Brown University Clinical Psychology Training Consortium. She is the recipient of a Career Development Award from the National Institute of Mental Health to examine parent–child interaction patterns and temperamental factors that may be associated with anxiety disorders in children. Clinically, she specializes in cognitive-behavioral treatment for children and adolescents with anxiety disorders. Dr. Garcia has served as co-investigator on several treatment outcome studies for children and adolescents with obsessive-compulsive disorder. Dr. Garcia has presented and published articles on childhood anxiety disorders and OCD in youth.

CPSIA information can be obtained at www.ICGtesting.com
Printed in the USA
BVOW01s1239161014

371054BV00002B/25/P